Arms Trafficking and Colombia

Kim Cragin • *Bruce Hoffman*

Prepared for the
Defense Intelligence Agency

Approved for public release;
distribution unlimited

RAND
National Defense Research Institute

The research described in this report was sponsored by the Defense Intelligence Agency. The research was conducted in RAND's National Defense Research Institute, a federally funded research and development center supported by the Office of the Secretary of Defense, the Joint Staff, the unified commands, and the defense agencies under Contract DASW01-01-C-0004.

Library of Congress Cataloging-in-Publication Data

Cragin, Kim.
    Arms trafficking and Colombia / Kim Cragin, Bruce Hoffman.
      p. cm.
    Includes bibliographical references.
    "MR-1468."
    ISBN 0-8330-3144-9 (pbk.)
    1. Illegal arms transfers—Colombia. 2. Arms transfers—Colombia. 3. Arms control. 4. Violence—Colombia. 5. Insurgency—Colombia. I. Hoffman, Bruce, 1954– II. Rand Corporation. III.Title.

    HD9743.C642C72 2003
    380.1'4562344'09861—dc21

                                      2003013085

Cover photograph by Bruce Hoffman

RAND is a nonprofit institution that helps improve policy and decisionmaking through research and analysis. RAND® is a registered trademark. RAND's publications do not necessarily reflect the opinions or policies of its research sponsors.

Cover design by Stephen Bloodsworth

Published 2003 by RAND
1700 Main Street, P.O. Box 2138, Santa Monica, CA 90407-2138
1200 South Hayes Street, Arlington, VA 22202-5050
201 North Craig Street, Suite 202, Pittsburgh, PA 15213-1516
RAND URL: http://www.rand.org/
To order RAND documents or to obtain additional information, contact Distribution Services: Telephone: (310) 451-7002; Fax: (310) 451-6915; Email: order@rand.org

PREFACE

The extent and type of weaponry currently available to terrorists, insurgents, and other criminals are enormous. These groups have exploited and developed local, regional, and global supply channels to traffic in munitions and equipment worldwide. Their access to weaponry is facilitated through covert transfers by governments and by legal and quasi-legal commercial dealers, outright black-market sales, and the theft or diversion of both state-owned and privately owned arms and weapons stores.

Small arms have a number of characteristics that contribute to their rapid and frequent movement across borders, between states, among various types of illegal organizations, and among certain entrepreneurial individuals. These types of weapons are by definition *lightweight*. This characteristic facilitates their cheap and easy transport, concealment, and covert movement. Arms shipments have been sent to terrorist and insurgent groups by boat, in trucks, on the backs of both humans and pack animals, and even through the mail. Light weapons are also relatively cheap, which opens up a very large potential buyer's market, even in the poorest parts of the world. Finally, light weapons are durable, requiring only a minimum level of field maintenance.

This report provides an analysis of black-market and gray-market sources of small arms, explosives, equipment, and materiel that are available to terrorist and insurgent organizations in Colombia. The authors pay particular attention to the sources and methods used by covert and/or illegal suppliers and purchasers to acquire, sell, buy, transfer, ship, and receive these items.

Information used in conducting this analysis was collected from January 1998 through September 2001.

This report should be of interest to policymakers as they attempt to determine the role that small-arms trafficking plays in internal conflicts. This report may also contribute to discussions on how to assess the internal decisionmaking processes of militant organizations.

The work documented here was conducted for the Defense Intelligence Agency, Terrorism Analysis Division within the International Security and Defense Policy Center of RAND's National Defense Research Institute, a federally funded research and development center sponsored by the Office of the Secretary of Defense, the Joint Staff, the unified commands, and the defense agencies.

Comments on this report are welcome and may be directed to either of the authors: Kim Cragin at cragin@rand.org or Bruce Hoffman at hoffman@rand.org.

CONTENTS

FIGURES

TABLE

The people of Colombia have experienced significant political in stability and violence over the past century. While many factors have contributed to this situation—the drug trade, a protracted insurgent conflict, nationwide corruption—small-arms proliferation remains among the most serious of the country's problems. Addressing the issue of small-arms trafficking in Colombia poses enormous challenges, largely because the movement of these weapons is difficult to monitor and measure and does not conform to traditional definitions of a security threat.

For this analysis, the term "small arms" refers to man-portable personal and military weapons, ranging from handguns to assault rifles to surface-to-air missiles (SAMs). These weapons are defined as *small arms* because they possess a number of characteristics that facilitate their rapid movement around the world. They are, by definition, small (and light), which allows for easy transportation across national borders and between continents. Small arms are also for the most part impervious to the environment, which allows for their repeated use in a wide range of climates and circumstances. Finally, small arms exist in legal white markets, semi-legal gray markets, and illegal black markets—resulting in a plethora of ways in which states and nonstate actors can access and distribute these arms.[1]

---

[1] Small arms are purchased in three different markets: white, gray, and black. White markets for military weapons include weapons bought and sold by authorized private manufacturers or state-owned enterprises. Gray markets occupy the space between white-market activities and the illegal trade in small arms. In the gray market, a state may arrange for an arms transfer to an illegitimate actor for political or economic pur-

Small-arms trafficking patterns can serve as a useful tool for analyzing political violence in two major ways: First, they can pinpoint specific weapons flows and networks—many of which mirror emerging zones of conflict; second, they can provide insight on the behavior of particular groups and their intentions. The second point is particularly true of ammunition—supplies of ammunition tend to be depleted far more rapidly than weapons stocks and, therefore, need to be replaced on a more consistent basis. In short, examining the specific manner by which arms and munitions are acquired and distributed may provide real-time information about the strategies behind a particular conflict and its likely future evolution.

PATTERNS OF ARMS TRAFFICKING INTO COLOMBIA

An analysis of small-arms activity in Colombia can be broken down into three distinct categories: the users of the weapons, the external sources and transportation routes for these munitions, and internal trafficking patterns.

Weapons Users

Two main leftist guerrilla organizations currently exist in Colombia—the Fuerzas Armadas Revolucionarias de Colombia (FARC) or the Revolutionary Armed Forces of Colombia and the Ejército de Liberación Nacional (ELN) or the National Liberation Army. Both of these groups have stated their intentions to seize control of national power, although both groups have also submitted reform agendas as part of their on-again, off-again peace negotiations with the government of Colombia. Currently, both groups are preoccupied with consolidating, defending, and, where possible, extending their respective bases of territorial control. Sustained access to weapons and ammunition supplies is crucial to this objective and, particularly in the case of FARC, is widely regarded as being directly proportional to each group's organizational strength, power, and influence.

FARC has experienced rapid growth of its membership since the early 1990s and now has approximately 15,000 members (not includ-

---

poses, but conceal the transfer in legal channels. Black-market activities are completely illegal. These markets are more fully discussed in Chapter Five.

ing coca farmers who might directly or indirectly support FARC). Over this same period of time, the ELN lost recruitment momentum; it now has half as many members as FARC. The expansion of FARC has put stress on its logistical capabilities: New members require their own weapons and access to a consistent supply of ammunition, forcing FARC to explore new arms sources and distribution routes (described in the next section).

The general trend appears to be for guerrillas to purchase their weapons in small quantities, most of which are of the military-grade, 7.62-caliber variety; there is no reliable evidence at this point to confirm reports that the group has acquired surface-to-air missiles (SAMs). There have been signs, however, of a possible shift in FARC's purchasing patterns toward "bulk buying." While the extent of this change should not be overstated, it could indicate that the group is seeking to step up the scale of its insurgent violence, possibly in re-sponse to U.S. support for Plan Colombia, which FARC sees as a threat to its funding sources and a direct military threat to the orga-nization itself through the introduction of U.S. Blackhawk heli-copters in the region.[2]

Paramilitaries constitute a second user group for small arms in Colombia. The country's paramilitaries are organized under the aus-pices of a loosely networked conglomeration known as Autodefensas Unidas de Colombia (AUC) or the United Self-Defense Forces of Colombia. The paramilitaries actively oppose FARC and the ELN and operate primarily in areas where state military strength is perceived to be weak.

Like arms acquisitions by guerrillas, arms acquisitions by paramili-taries tend to be small scale. However, as with FARC, there have also been isolated instances of larger arms shipments being received by the AUC; again, this situation probably reflects a short-term effort to augment the group's supplies in response to a growing membership. Most of the AUC's arms are of the 5.62-caliber variety, although there

---

[2]According to a U.S. State Department Web site (http://www.state.gov/www/regions/wha/colombia/fs_000719_plancolombia.html), the government of Colombia devel-oped Plan Colombia in 1999 as an integrated strategy to meet the most pressing chal-lenges confronting Colombia today—promoting the peace process, combating the narcotics industry, reviving the Colombian economy, and strengthening the demo-cratic pillars of Colombian society. Plan Colombia is a $7.5 billion program.

are signs that the group is now switching to larger 7.62-caliber (.51mm) munitions. Reports indicate that the 7.62-caliber ammunition is easier to acquire in regional black markets, which may explain the shift. Additionally, this shift to larger-caliber munitions suggests that the AUC is also expanding its arms acquisition operations beyond its traditional sources, indicating designs by the AUC to counter heightened FARC activities.

Private citizens constitute the third user group for small arms in Colombia. Citizen demand for arms primarily reflects the endemic civil, political, and criminal violence that plagues the country, combined with a general lack of confidence in the state's overall institutional viability and authority. Most private citizens' arms acquisitions focus on personal weapons, such as revolvers and pistols, although military-style weapons are also periodically sought and traded.[3]

Arms trafficking is on an upward spiral among all three user groups, which has, in effect, contributed to an internal "arms race" in Colombia. FARC and the ELN buy weapons to attack the existing government and to challenge the government's monopoly on coercive force. These actions by FARC and the ELN cause the AUC to step up its own acquisition initiatives to counter the guerrillas, which, in turn feeds into the heightened civil violence and prompts private citizens to increase their own gun purchases for personal protection. Thus, while small arms have always been part of the political conflict in Colombia, the current arms trafficking situation is much more intense and dynamic than in the past, and it now affects virtually every aspect of Colombia's rural and urban life.

External Sources and Transportation Routes

Several factors contribute to the rapid and relatively free flow of small arms into Colombia, including its position as a geographic bridge between Central and South America, borders that are

---

[3]Criminals and transnational criminal organizations also contribute to a demand for small arms in Colombia. In this analysis, criminals are interpreted as being either (1) normal citizens seeking to purchase weapons; (2) suppliers of weapons on Colombia's internal market; or (3) facilitators of weapons purchases for paramilitary and guerrilla organizations in the international market. The analysis does not, however, specifically focus on criminal acquisition patterns.

"porous" and difficult to monitor, a government presence that is mostly concentrated in the cities of the Andean mountains and that is essentially nonexistent in southern Colombia, and marine outlets that provide access to both the Caribbean Sea and the Pacific Ocean. The arms flow problem is further magnified by the availability of Cold War–era weapons stockpiles in Nicaragua, Honduras, and El Salvador and the alleged assistance of regional sympathizers in Cuba and Venezuela.

Most small arms appear to move from external sources into Colombia through black-market routes.[4] Weapons are rarely trafficked or purchased in bulk; rather, weapons "trickle" into Colombia by ones or twos, or perhaps by the dozen. Cumulatively, however, these shipments can amount to a substantial volume of arms during the course of just a single year.

Central America represents the single largest source of illegal weapons to Colombia, with five countries—El Salvador, Honduras, Nicaragua, Panama, and Costa Rica—accounting for more than a third of all arms shipped into the country. Similarly, former Cold War conflict zones (notably Nicaragua, El Salvador, and Guatemala) have become a "magnet" for small-arms dealers, as witnessed by the proliferation of unscrupulous entrepreneurs who acquire and sell arms to paramilitaries and guerrillas alike, depending on who is the highest bidder.

In addition to being a source for small arms, Central America also acts as an important transit route. From 1998 to 2001, Panama was the single largest transshipment point for weapons into Colombia. Munitions are smuggled out of Panama either by land (mostly across the densely forested Darien Gap), by sea (generally via the Pacific seaboard in the case of FARC or Caribbean ports in the case of the AUC), or by air (with most flights destined for Magdalena or Choco). Currently, an estimated 50 percent of all illegal weapons arriving in Colombia by sea are trafficked through Panama.

---

[4]We collected information on small-arms trafficking from January 1998 through September 2001. The figures in this report all stem from that collection effort. During that period, more than 75 percent of the illegal small-arms trafficking in Colombia originated outside of the country. See the Appendix for more details.

Honduras and Nicaragua also constitute important routing hubs, especially for arms originating in El Salvador. The three most important collection and distribution points in these two countries are Catacamas in Honduras and Eteli and Managua in Nicaragua. Although Costa Rica is not as important a routing hub as Panama, Honduras, or Nicaragua, statistically significant flows of arms pass through Costa Rica, with most weapons originating in Los Chiles (which borders Nicaragua), Puerto Armuelles (which borders Panama), or Santa Ana (which lies on the Guatemala–El Salvador border).

Outside of information pertaining to Panama, there is very little detailed information on the transportation methods used to smuggle weapons into Colombia from Central America. However, on the basis of the general terrain and types of port cities in Central America, it would appear that most arms are brought into Colombia by either motorboats designed to navigate in shallow waters or small fishing vessels. If land routes are chosen, traffickers seem to focus on hiding weapons and ammunition within legitimate shipments of produce, such as potatoes and cereal, as they are being transported to towns for sale. The significance of these smuggling patterns is that they lend themselves to small-scale activity and preclude the need for forged user-end certificates, sophisticated coverups, or any other method typically used by state-sponsored traffickers or criminal syndicates to illegally transport arms. This type of activity would suggest that effective interdiction of weapon flows from Central America into Colombia requires a more active, targeted, systematic, and strategic policy than the general international monitoring regulations and/or enforcement.

Colombia's immediate neighbors (Venezuela, Brazil, Peru, Ecuador, and Panama) all act as both sources and transit routes for small-arms trafficking. However, these states are not equipped with caches of available weapons the size of those that exist in Nicaragua, Honduras, and El Salvador. As a result, traffickers typically purchase weapons from criminal organizations, obtain them from legal markets, bribe private security forces, or raid government military stockpiles.

Venezuela, Brazil, Peru, and Ecuador act as source countries for small arms in South America. Munitions moving from Venezuela generally include black-market items that have circuitously traveled from Mexico, Israel, Brazil, or Spain. Certain weapons have also been traced back to the Venezuelan armed forces. Although there is no definitive evidence at this point that links the administration of Venezuelan President Hugo Chavez to a deliberate policy of arming Colombia's guerrillas, it is possible that sympathetic individual members of the Venezuelan military have supplied both weapons and ammunition to FARC and the ELN.

Most guns from Brazil are thought to originate from the Iguazu Falls. This area is part of the so-called "tri-border" region that links Argentina, Paraguay, and Brazil, and which is a well-known source for weapons, drugs, and money laundering. FARC agents have also been arrested in Tabatinga (Brazil) and Leticia (Colombia), which together form a pivotal point for black-market activity in general and arms trafficking in particular.

Arms flowing into Colombia from Ecuador and Peru emanate mostly from stolen military stocks or supplies that have been illegally resold by members of private security firms. In the case of Ecuador, individual citizens have been known to inject weapons into the Colombian black market either for direct profit or as partial payment for kidnap ransoms.

The most significant role that Colombia's Latin American neighbors play in arms trafficking, however, is as transshipment and transit points. Supplies enter Colombia by several means and via a number of collection and distribution hubs. Land routes provide the guerrillas with their most constant supply of small arms, with most flows of arms crossing over the densely forested and swampy Venezuelan, Ecuadorian, and Brazilian borders, either by road (in the case of Venezuela and Ecuador) or by river (in the case of Brazil).

Weapons shipments that come into Colombia by air and by sea are generally grouped together in larger bundles than those transported over land. Traffickers primarily use fishing vessels to transport weapons directly into Pacific or Caribbean ports, although they also occasionally pack arms in plastic bags and drop them offshore for later collection by smaller boats, which then transport the arms to prearranged destinations, such as inlets and coves. While Panama accounts for the bulk of shipments that come in by sea, significant volumes are also smuggled from Ecuador. The main travel route for those shipments is from Esmeraldes (Ecuador) to the Colombian Pacific ports of Tumaco and Buenaventura.

Just under a half of all illegal weapons that arrive in Colombia by air are flown in planes departing from Brazil. Munitions are generally flown, either directly or via Suriname, to small landing strips in FARC's demilitarized zone (DMZ)[5]—five FARC-controlled munici-palities in south-central Colombia—or to the Guainia and Vichada Departments.[6] Mostly small, single-engine charter planes, each of which is able to carry up to one ton of cargo, are used to transport the arms. In terms of numbers of weapons, this equates to approximately 100 AK-47s, not including ammunition.

FARC and the AUC are striving for consistency in their arms ship-ments from external sources. Both groups are currently fighting for control of regions in Colombia that provide the best access to land and sea routes and have explored relationships with criminal organi-zations to negotiate "bulk purchases." High-volume purchases, how-ever, remain the exception to the rule, with most weapons from Central and Latin America continuing to trickle into Colombia through black markets.

PATTERNS OF ARMS TRAFFICKING INSIDE COLOMBIA

Most of the illegal small arms that originate from inside Colombia's borders are stolen from production facilities or are sold through the black market by Colombia's security forces. Many of these weapons have been traced to Industria Militar (Indumil), the main manufac-turing company that produces munitions for the Colombian security forces. Arms are either stolen and then sold by factory workers and guards or are directly raided from government storehouses by FARC, the ELN, or the AUC themselves. Military personnel sympathetic to the aims of either the guerrillas or (especially) the self-defense mili-tias are also known to have illegally distributed assault weapons and ammunition, demonstrating at least a limited interaction between Colombia's security forces and the country's internal black market.

---

[5]As of January 2002, the DMZ is no longer in existence.

[6]A Colombian *department* is a political division akin to a state or province.

Three primary smuggling routes exist in Colombia. The first uses water and land routes to transport weapons from Ocana, via Cucuta and Pamplona, to Bucaramanga and Barrancabermeja. The second runs from the Gulf of Uraba (located near the border with Panama), along the Chigorodo-Dabeiba highway to Medellín. The third draws on an inner-city patchwork of collection and distribution hubs that have formed within the capital city of Bogotá and that feed market neighborhoods in San Victorino, El Cartucho, Patio Bonito, Cuidad Bolivar, and Corabastos. Most of the traffickers within the capital operate in small cells of no more than ten members who take and fill orders directly on the streets or, in the case of more-complicated requests, via messenger services.

SECURITY AND POLICY IMPLICATIONS

For at least two reasons, the proliferation of small arms in Colombia is directly relevant to the United States:

First, FARC is one of the largest and most well-funded militant organizations in the world. Although FARC has engaged primarily in guerrilla warfare within Colombia's rural regions, since 2002 the group has increased its capability to conduct attacks on major cities. With the advent of the "war on terrorism," FARC could focus more attention on U.S. targets. Moreover, our analysis demonstrates that FARC was able to supply its rapidly expanding membership with weapons relatively easily from 1998 through 2001 (the period of this study). This expansion appears to be closely correlated to perceived increased threats, as discussed above, from the U.S.-backed Plan Colombia. Thus, we conclude that FARC has the resources and ability to strategically manage its weapons supplies and could pose a threat to the United States should it choose to do so.

Second, small-arms transfers have had a negative impact on regional stability in Latin America. Ready access to weapons has helped to both entrench and empower guerrilla and paramilitary forces in Colombia. Not only has this situation threatened the security of the fourth-largest economy in Latin America, it has also triggered highly deleterious cross-border flows of refugees, drugs, and violence that have already had a negative impact on Panama, Venezuela, Brazil, Peru, and Ecuador.

ACKNOWLEDGMENTS

The authors would like to thank the sponsors of this study within the Defense Intelligence Agency for their interest and assistance in our work. The research presented in this report also benefited greatly from the contributions of Michael McNicholas from the Phoenix Group, Peter Chalk of RAND, and Aaron Padilla of the University of Cambridge. Additional critical logistical assistance was provided by Security and Intelligence Advising, a private international security firm. The authors are indebted to the firm's president, Amar Salman, for facilitating our June 2001 research trip to Colombia. Needless to say, however, any errors or omissions are the responsibility of the authors.

Finally, many individuals inside Colombia and Argentina contributed significantly to this analysis. They provided information on illegal trafficking patterns and a context for the political violence inside Colombia. At their request, we have not mentioned these individuals or their organizations by name. Nevertheless, we do want to acknowledge the nongovernmental organizations, academics, and security officials in Colombia who are faced with the problem of illegal arms trafficking every day. We hope that these individuals will find this report worthy of their time and help, and that one day Colombia will truly achieve peace.

ATF	U.S. Bureau of Alcohol, Tobacco, and Firearms
AUC	Autodefensas Unidas de Colombia (United Self-Defense Forces of Colombia)
DMZ	Demilitarized zone
ELN	Ejército de Liberación Nacional (National Liberation Army) (Colombia)
ETA	Euskadi ta Askatasuna (Basque region)
FARC	Fuerzas Armadas Revolucionarias de Colombia (Revolutionary Armed Forces of Colombia)
FMLN	Frente Farabundo Martí para la Liberación Nacional (Farabundo Marti National Liberation Front) (El Salvador)
Indumil	Industria Militar (Colombia)
IRA	Irish Republican Army
NGO	Nongovernmental organization
SAM	Surface-to-air missile
U.N.	United Nations

Political Map of Colombia

Chapter One

INTRODUCTION

The people of Colombia live in the midst of violent crime and political revolution. Although the source of this instability may not be obvious, it nevertheless affects the everyday activities of ordinary individuals. The violence comes in the form of theft, kidnapping, murder, and guerrilla assaults. It affects the poor farmer, the teacher, the banker, and the rich industrialist alike. And behind all of this violence is small-arms trafficking.

This report follows two distinct analytical threads:

First, we examine the scope and dimensions of small-arms trafficking into and within Colombia. In Chapters Two through Four, we identify the weapons sources and routes used by traffickers to transport weapons into the country.[1] We also examine the various guerrilla groups, paramilitaries, criminals, and ordinary citizens who purchase and use these munitions. However, these chapters focus primarily on small arms and light weapons acquired by guerrillas and paramilitaries for the purpose of confronting the Colombian state.

Second, we examine Colombia's political conflict through the lens of small-arms trafficking. In Chapters Five and Six, we explore the interaction among Colombia's guerrillas, paramilitaries, security forces, criminals, and average citizens. Chapter Six concludes with policy implications for the U.S. government.

---

[1] We collected information on small-arms trafficking from January 1998 through September 2001.

At the core of both lines of analysis lies the question of how state governments in general can control their domestic security in the face of increasingly transnational threats. This issue is explored in Chapter Five, in which we argue that small-arms trafficking patterns provide an interesting framework for addressing this challenge.

At first glance, solving the problem of illegal weapons use in a society such as Colombia's would appear to be a simple matter of tightening internal regulations. However, weapons are becoming increasingly easy to move across borders, and like other nonperishable commodities, weapons can be resold and recycled. Indeed, the cyclical nature of small-arms trafficking is precisely what makes it an issue affecting *regional* and not just national stability. Confronting the challenge of illegal arms trafficking is problematic, largely because small-arms trafficking does not conform to traditional definitions of a security threat. This report attempts to put forth a first step toward finding a solution to this difficult problem.

Chapter Two

VIOLENCE IN COLOMBIA

The Colombian domestic landscape has been marked by significant political, social, and economic upheavals in the 20th century. These upheavals have led to the emergence of a number of substate groups challenging the authority and power of the Bogotá government, all of whom have generated a rising demand for illegal small arms. Exacerbating the situation is Colombia's physical geography, which is highly conducive to the illegal trafficking of weapons into and throughout the country. Finally, a number of geopolitical issues have magnified the problem of arms smuggling in Colombia and serve to illustrate the context in which countries typically operate when they try to deal with global political and criminal problems locally.

COLOMBIA'S POLITICAL CONFLICT

The current fighting in Colombia is grounded in class wars rather than in religious or ethnic conflicts. Colombian newspapers have referred to this fighting as "la Violencia," a term that was originally used to describe the period of social revolution in Colombia from 1948 to 1974.[1] The term "la Violencia" has been appropriated of late to identify more-recent periods of tremendous instability and conflict in Colombia. While the objective of our analysis is not to reiterate the historical evolution of la Violencia, we do contend that small-arms trafficking patterns reveal oft-hidden characteristics of this

---

[1]Arnson, Cynthia, ed., *Comparative Peace Processes in Latin America*, Washington, D.C.: Woodrow Wilson Center Press, 1999, pp. 159–204.

political conflict. This position necessitates a brief discussion of the background of Colombia's political conflict.

Colombia's Guerrilla Organizations: FARC and the ELN

> Although it may seem paradoxical, the war with its cruelties and pain is the only possible remedy to break the terror of the strong against the weak. . . . Coming from this, the paradoxical relationship between war and peace, as complements, as derived one from the other, as an integral part of the historical course that, instead of putting us in opposition binds us, unites us, puts us together. To make war in order to achieve peace with social justice is the summary of this binomial interrelationship (statement of the National Liberation Army, 1998).[2]

Two left-wing guerrilla organizations operate inside Colombia's borders—Fuerzas Armadas Revolucionarias de Colombia (FARC) or Revolutionary Armed Forces of Colombia and Ejército de Liberación Nacional (ELN) or National Liberation Army. The FARC controls territory in Colombia's sparsely populated south. It derives its base of support from peasant farmers or *campesinos* and its pro-revolution rhetoric from the politics of the peasant population. FARC's organization and modus operandi follow that of most guerrilla groups. FARC is divided into a number of different "fronts," which function as military-like units. These organizational subdivisions are given a certain degree of independence in their operations, but also receive general guidance from a central FARC secretariat, which also assigns the units specific responsibilities.[3]

Most analyses of FARC include a series of maps with colored dots marking the location of the group's various fronts. These cartographical aids do not, however, provide much insight into the internal de-

---

[2]Translated from "La Paz Sobre La Mesa," *Cambio*, Special Edition, May 11, 1998, p. 22.

[3]For example, Front 57 maintains FARC's drug trafficking and logistical bases in Panama's Darien Gap, and Front 16 is responsible for securing financial transactions. Some fronts are also assigned to a particular department in Colombia, while others conduct mobile operations. From author interviews, Bogotá, June 2000; McNicholas, Michael, *Colombian Guerrilla and Para-Military Arms Procurement: Origin and Routes*, Panama City: Phoenix Group, 2001; "Armas Por Coca," *Cambio*, July 12, 1999, p. 30.

cisionmaking structure and operations of FARC. Indeed, the actual organizational structure of FARC is fairly opaque. Subsequent chapters attempt to illuminate FARC's organization by outlining the tactical sophistication, strategic objectives, and intentions of FARC as revealed by small-arms trafficking patterns into and within Colombia.

FARC first funded its operations against Colombia's security forces by kidnapping rich landowners and then demanding ransom for their release. Originally opposed to narcotics trafficking, FARC changed its position on narcotics during the 1980s and began to both encourage and tax coca cultivation.[4] FARC's participation in the drug trade allowed it to simultaneously increase its revenues and maintain the support of coca-growing farmers, enabling the group to attract increasing numbers of fighters.

Current estimates of FARC membership and revenues range from approximately 15,000 to 17,500 armed members and $250 million to $600 million in annual revenues.[5] In August 2000, the Colombian newsweekly, *Semana*, published the agenda from an annual meeting of the FARC secretariat. The agenda included the following statement: "The acquisition of arms currently has permitted us a qualitative jump in our process of becoming the Ejército del Pueblo ['Army of the People' or FARC-EP]."[6] This statement is important because it illustrates the strong psychological connection FARC leadership made between weapons and power. To FARC, a demonstrated increase in its weapons and ammunition is directly proportional to its overall strength, power, and influence. This correlation was reinforced when FARC's units crushed the Colombian Armed Forces in a

---

[4]Rabasa, Angel, and Peter Chalk, *Colombian Labyrinth: The Synergy of Drugs and Insurgency and Its Implications for Regional Stability*, Santa Monica, Calif.: RAND, MR-1339, 2001, pp. 25–26.

[5]"Los Costos Del Cese Al Fuego," *El País*, July 6, 2000. U.S. sources tend to lean toward the higher estimates, with local Colombian sources consistently citing lower numbers for both FARC members and income.

[6]The "qualitative jump" mentioned by FARC may reflect more rhetoric than reality. Chapter Four discusses reports that indicate FARC does not have as many weapons as its public comments such as this one imply ("Los Planes De Las Farc," *Semana*, August 7, 2000, p. 35).

series of battles in Las Delicias, Puerres, el Billar, Miraflores, and Mitú in 1997 and 1998.[7]

The ELN is another left-wing guerrilla group in Colombia. It primarily operates in the oil-producing departments[8] and northeastern cities of the country. Unlike FARC, the ELN is not a peasant-based revolutionary movement. Rather, it is a Marxist-Leninist group with origins in the country's university campuses. As a result, the ELN's social base is not as broad as FARC's. The group largely targets oil pipelines in its guerrilla attacks in an effort to discourage the presence of multinationals in Colombia, and blames the multinational companies for exploiting Colombia's natural resources to the detriment of local communities. Most of the ELN's enmity in this regard is directed toward U.S. companies operating in the region. Reflecting these attitudes, the ELN's terms for peace negotiations, which were publicized in 1998 in Geneva, stated that any dialogue must "put in motion a patriotic conduct of sovereignty, national self-determination and independence vis-à-vis the United States, other imperialists, and transnational businesses, gaining our own conception of national sovereignty."[9] The ELN is still a relatively minor player in Colombia's political conflict, however, and has less than half the number of members that FARC has. As such, our analysis focuses primarily on FARC.

Colombia's Paramilitary Organization: The AUC

The Autodefensas Unidas de Colombia (AUC) or United Self-Defense Forces of Colombia is a conglomeration of paramilitary organizations operating throughout Colombia. Like the guerrilla groups, the AUC is active in drug-producing areas of the country. Along with other local militias, the AUC also fights against the guerrillas, especially in areas where the Colombian military has less of a presence.

The AUC maintains a strong presence in northeastern Colombia and the city of Barrancabermeja, although it has also challenged FARC and the ELN within a number of their strongholds, including the

---

[7]Padilla, Nelson Freddy, "Cabañuelas De Paz," *Cambio*, December 21, 1998, pp. 24–25.

[8]A Colombian *department* is a political division akin to a state or province.

[9]"La Paz Sobre La Mesa," 1998, p. 33.

Antioquia and Chocó Departments and the city of Buenaventura. Membership in the AUC expanded rapidly between 1999 and 2001 (the years of this study), mostly as a result of its successful encounters with FARC. AUC has approximately 8,500 armed members, some of whom stay confined within the traditional AUC strongholds while others are challenging FARC and the ELN to an increasingly greater degree within the two guerrilla groups' strongholds.[10]

The AUC has argued for its own place at the negotiating table occupied by the guerrillas and Colombian government in an attempt to obtain a share of political power.[11] Like FARC and the ELN, the AUC derives taxes from coca cultivation. It also earns money from private landowners (ranchers) who pay the AUC to protect them from kidnappings by guerrillas. Therefore, the AUC has a financial incentive for the current fighting in Colombia to continue. Paramilitary groups affiliated with the AUC search out and kill campesinos whom they accuse of collaborating with FARC. This is the AUC's way of establishing authority over a village, thereby strengthening its claim to a seat at the negotiating table.[12]

Colombia's Citizens

Previous waves of internal violence rarely affected Colombia's middle class. The guerrillas kidnapped members of the social elite, and the security forces fought the guerrillas in remote rural areas, populated by the campesinos and the lower classes. Indeed, until recently, the majority of Colombia's population did not regularly experience violence. This situation changed in the 1990s. FARC and the ELN are now increasingly kidnapping and/or threatening members of the middle class.[13] In 2000, there were approximately ten kidnappings per day in Colombia.[14] Additionally, it is not uncommon for individ-

---

[10]The AUC has also been able to draft former guerrillas and even ex-soldiers from the Colombian military (Wilson, Scott, "Interview with Carlos Castano, Head of the United Self-Defense Forces of Colombia," *Washington Post*, March 12, 2001b).

[11]"La Paz Sobre La Mesa," 1998.

[12]Wilson, 2001b.

[13]Author interviews, Bogotá, April 2001; "El Otro Plan Colombia," *Cambio*, March 20, 2000, pp. 25–26, "Farc Se Movilizan Al Sur De Bolívar," *El Tiempo*, July 16, 2001.

[14]"El Otro Plan Colombia," 2000, p. 24.

ual citizens to receive a phone call telling them that they are required to pay a "10 percent tax" to support Colombia's revolution. Guerrillas reportedly just go through the phone book, much like telemarketers in the United States.[15]

Criminal activity has also increased in Colombia. In 1983, the country experienced an annual homicide rate of 24 for every 100,000 people. In 1993, the rate increased to 88 for every 100,000 people.[16] Currently, 30,000 people are murdered in Colombia each year in addition to those killed in the political conflict. This equates to almost 100 deaths per 100,000 people.[17] In the United States, a homicide rate of this magnitude would calculate to approximately 285,000 deaths per year from criminal violence, as compared with the 18,000 deaths from criminal violence that occur annually (according to 1998 figures).[18]

Everyday citizens in Colombia, therefore, feel threatened by violent political and criminal activities. So, they buy guns. Approximately 165,000 residents of Bogotá alone own *legal* personal weapons.[19] This figure does not even account for the robust illegal market in Bogotá (see Chapter Four). In response to this increased demand for weapons, Colombia's three major cities—Calí, Medellín, and Bogotá—have implemented various forms of weapons decommissioning and buy-back initiatives. The most advanced of these programs is a program run in Bogotá in which the 13th Brigade of the Colombian Army helps police to confiscate illegal guns and ammunition.[20] The overall effectiveness of the scheme has been severely constrained, however, by the fact that as many as 30 to 40 percent of

---

[15]Author interviews, Bogotá, April 2001; "El Otro Plan Colombia," 2000, p. 25.

[16]Villaveces, Andres, et al., "Effect of a Ban on Carrying Firearms on Homicide Rates in Two Colombian Cities," *Journal of the American Medical Association*, Vol. 283, No. 9, 2000, p. 1205.

[17]Jenkins, Brian Michael, "Colombia: Crossing a Dangerous Threshold," *The National Interest*, 2000, p. 48.

[18]Chauvin, Lucien, and Juan Tamayo, "Peru, Colombia Want U.S. to Resume Anti-Drug Support," *Miami Herald*, August 4, 2001; "Traicion En El Mercado Negro De Armas," *El Tiempo*, June 28, 2000.

[19]Selsky, Andrew, "Colombian Rebel Unit Routed in Ground, Air Counterattack," *Miami Herald*, August 3, 2001.

[20]Author interviews, Bogotá city official, June 2001.

the apprehended weapons are sold back to the public.[21] As such, even the most robust decommissioning program in Colombia has had a questionable impact on the weapons market, and the monitoring of these decommissioned guns fluctuates periodically. As a result, there is little disincentive for individuals to purchase either legal or illegal guns.

Colombia's Internal Arms Race

The country's three principal nonstate actors—guerrillas, paramilitaries, and ordinary citizens—stimulate the demand for small arms.[22] The misuse of these weapons is a major problem that Colombian society faces in the midst of political conflict and crime; however, the acquisition and use of small arms provides an interesting insight into the three nonstate actors.

From 1998 to 2001 (the period of this study), there appeared to be an "arms race" in Colombia. FARC acquired weapons to attack the existing government, the paramilitary groups purchased arms to challenge FARC, and citizens bought guns to protect themselves from both kidnappings and random violence in rural areas. The most interesting aspect of this situation is the absence of the Colombian security forces. Of course, these security forces are significant players in the ongoing conflict. But citizens have behaved as if the Colombian military and police cannot protect them. In the past, only campesinos and wealthy landowners compensated for their lack of protection by acquiescing to demands from insurgents or by obtaining weapons to use themselves. But now, this phenomenon has spread to Colombia's cities and affected its middle class. So, while small arms have always been a part of the political conflict, in recent years the situation has intensified and taken on all the characteristics of an arms race.

---

[21]Author interviews, Bogotá city official, June 2001.

[22]Criminals and transnational criminal organizations also contribute to a demand for small arms in Colombia. In this analysis, criminals are interpreted as being either (1) normal citizens seeking to purchase weapons; (2) suppliers of weapons on Colombia's internal market; or (3) facilitators of weapons purchases for paramilitary and guerrilla organizations in the international market. The analysis does not, however, specifically focus on criminal acquisition patterns.

COLOMBIA'S PHYSICAL GEOGRAPHY

Colombia's physical geography contributes to its rapid influx of small arms. Colombia's cities are located in the Andean mountains, which bisect the country from north to south (see the map facing page 1). Most of the country's population is concentrated in the urban centers, while the rural southeastern portion of the country is sparsely populated and remains underdeveloped. This is precisely the area controlled by FARC. The Colombian government has rarely had a solid presence in the rural southeast, focusing its governance and economic development efforts on the cities in the Andean mountains. As a result, over the years, FARC has been able to build operational and logistics bases in southern Colombia that it has used for storing weapons.

Moreover, Colombia's borders with Panama, Ecuador, Peru, and Brazil are covered with dense forests, which prohibit commercial traffic except via the major highways. Colombia's armed forces have not been able to secure these borders, which has allowed FARC to build its own road to transport fuel and other medical supplies from Ecuador into Colombia. Additionally, Colombia's borders with Venezuela and Brazil have terrain with both swamps and rivers, which allow traffickers to effectively transport illegal commodities without detection. In October 2000, a federal police agent from Brazil commented on the difficulties presented by his country bordering Colombia: "Even if we had 10 times more men or 100 times more men, it would still be very hard to police the frontier because it is so extensive."[23]

COLOMBIA'S GEOPOLITICAL CHARACTERISTICS

Three geopolitical characteristics of Colombia—the availability of post–Cold War arms stockpiles, the country's demilitarized zones, and potential state interference—magnify the problem of small-arms trafficking into Colombia. These characteristics affect arms trafficking patterns (i.e., arms users, arms sources, and trafficking routes)

---

[23]Dyer, Geoff, "Time Bomb at Brazil Outpost," *Financial Times*, Internet edition, October 3, 2000.

and the efficacy of any policy recommendation designed to address the arms trafficking problem.[24]

Characteristic 1: The Availability of Arms Stockpiles

Stockpiles of arms dating back to the Cold War, which were originally provided to various combatants in Latin America by the United States and the former Soviet Union, are still readily accessible. During the 1970s and 1980s, the United States, Cuba, and the Soviet Union aggressively sought to promote their ideological agendas in the Americas. One of the most publicized events resulting from the Cold War–era ideological struggle in Latin America was the Iran-Contra Affair. One element of this covert operation involved the U.S. military transferring small arms to Nicaragua, Honduras, and El Salvador. But most of these munitions were not M-16s produced by the U.S. arms industry, for example, but rather weapons manufactured in Soviet-bloc countries (e.g., Kalashnikov AK-47 assault rifles). Information produced during the Iran-Contra hearings revealed that small arms were frequently shipped into Central America from the United States during the Cold War, and these shipments typically included approximately 20,000 to 75,000 pounds of small arms and ammunition.[25] Many of these weapons are still available throughout Latin America.[26]

---

[24] It should be noted that these characteristics are not completely unique to Colombia. Indeed, these circumstances illuminate common problems facing many other countries affected by small-arms trafficking. For example, Bosnia's proximity to former Soviet Bloc stockpiles contributes to its influx of arms. Likewise, contentiousness over territorial borders in Kashmir and Afghanistan has created zones similar to Colombia's demilitarized zone (DMZ) that encourage black-market activity.

[25] Klare, Michael, and David Andersen, *A Scourge of Guns: The Diffusion of Small Arms and Light Weapons in Latin America*, Washington, D.C.: Federation of American Scientists/Arms Sales Monitoring Project, 1996, p. 81.

[26] It is also true that many of the weapons in Latin America have been accessed from black markets in conflict zones such as Bosnia. As such, it is difficult from an analytical viewpoint to gauge the extent of the arms caches that are still in Central America and to then attribute the source of these stockpiles to either past transfers or contemporary transactions. Nonetheless, publicly available information (e.g., Klare and Andersen [1996]) does indicate that Cold War–era shipments easily equate to tens of thousands of small arms and ammunition for those arms, and that those arms constitute an important component of Latin America's black market.

With the end of the conflict in El Salvador, Honduras, Guatemala, and Nicaragua during the 1990s, the United Nations and a few select European countries sponsored decommissioning and collection programs to remove small arms from open circulation in Central America. Table 2.1 lists the number of weapons collected via these initiatives and compares those numbers with the number of combatants per country.[27] The information in the table supports our contention that thousands, or even tens of thousands, of weapons likely remain in caches throughout Central America.

The geographical proximity of these weapons caches to Colombia makes it easy for traffickers to meet the demand generated by the country's internal conflict. Central America is linked to Colombia by the Pan-American Highway, and even though this highway terminates at Panama's Darien Gap, small fishing vessels and planes travel the distance between Panama and Colombia on a regular basis. Furthermore, the governments of Central America do not have adequate security force capabilities to tackle the problem of small-arms trafficking. Costa Rica and Panama, in particular, lack military forces

Table 2.1

Weapons Decommissioned in Central America, as of 2000

	Nicaragua	Honduras	El Salvador	Total
Estimated combatants	52,000	N/A	40,000	92,000
Small arms destroyed/ decommissioned	78,408	512	8,876	97,695
Grenades destroyed/ decommissioned	740	570	12,408	13,718
Missiles destroyed/ decommissioned	82	30	75	187

N/A = Not applicable.

---

[27]Arnson, 1999, pp. 31–57; Klare and Anderson, 1996; Lock, Peter, "Breaking the Cycle of Violence: Light Weapons Destruction in Central America," in *BASIC PAPERS* series, London, UK: British American Security Information Council, 1997; and Laurance, Edward, and William Godnick, "Weapons Collection in Central America: El Salvador and Guatemala," in *Managing the Remnants of War: Weapons Collection and Disposal as an Element of Peace-Building*, Bonn, Germany: Bonn International Center for Conversion, 2000. The authors of this report also verified this information through interviews with U.S. government officials.

and are, therefore, woefully underequipped to help Colombia reduce the available small arms stockpiled in and flowing through their countries on their way to Colombia.

Partly in reaction to this situation, in 1998 Colombia joined 25 other countries from around the world to establish a network of state security apparatuses linked to Interpol and the U.S. Bureau of Alcohol, Tobacco, and Firearms (ATF) to counter illegal small-arms trafficking.[28] While networks such as this will provide transit countries with the intelligence resources they need to track the flow of small arms from existing stockpiles through their country, these networks do not provide transit countries with the critical strategic resources they need to destroy caches at their source. At this point, there is no fully resourced international initiative or mechanism that can be used to help countries discover and eliminate stockpiles of Cold War–era weapons within their borders.

Characteristic 2: Colombia's Demilitarized Zone (1998–2001)

On November 6, 1998, former Colombian President Andres Pastrana demilitarized five FARC-controlled municipalities in south-central Colombia, creating an area known as the demilitarized zone (DMZ) (see Figure 2.1). (As of January 2002, the DMZ is no longer in existence.) The goal of the DMZ was to provide an incentive and create a political as well as territorial space for negotiations between the government of Colombia and FARC.[29] Yet, FARC transformed the DMZ into a logistical hub that was highly beneficial for the organization for stockpiling weapons, ammunitions, and other supplies and for directing attacks against the Colombian military.[30]

---

[28]"Bloque De 25 Paises Contra El Mercado Negro De Armas," *El Tiempo*, May 8, 1998.

[29]FARC's demands included land reform and a reduction in the presence of multinational companies, and FARC made broad statements on political reform to include stronger popular participatory measures (Serafino, Nina M., *Colombia: Conditions and U.S. Policy Options*, Washington, D.C.: Congressional Research Service, RL 30330, 1999, p. 32).

[30]For a discussion on FARC administration of the DMZ, see "El Gobierno De Las Farc," *Semana*, January 25, 1999.

Figure 2.1—Colombia's Demilitarized Zone (1998–2001)

Characteristic 3: Potential State Interference

Cuba has a history of supporting left-wing guerrilla organizations in Latin America, and this type of support also holds true for the guerrillas operating in Colombia. During peace negotiations in 1998, President Pastrana and the ELN established a group of friendly nations to act as supervisors of peace negotiations and intermediaries between the Colombian government and the guerrilla groups.[31] This group included a select number of European nations and Cuba, suggesting a belief that Havana wields significant influence over the ELN. However, it is difficult to gauge the level of Cuban involvement in arms acquisition by the ELN or FARC.

As just mentioned, Cuba has a long track record of supporting guerrilla groups, including the ELN and FARC. Furthermore, an arms shipment uncovered in 2000 was traced from France to Havana to the Isla Escuda de Veraguas in Colombia; it is suspected that this shipment eventually reached FARC in Puerto Obaldia.[32] It is not possible, however, to distinguish black-market activity transiting Havana from direct state support. A number of allegations also have been made in the Colombian press that Venezuelan President Hugo Chavez allows his military to provide logistical support to the ELN and FARC.[33] Chapter Three outlines the extent of this assistance, but, at this point, available information confirms only that sympathizers within Venezuela's armed forces are selling ammunition and weapons to the guerrillas on their own initiative.

Both the ELN and FARC are less dependent on potential state sponsors than guerrilla or terrorist groups elsewhere because of their heavy involvement in kidnapping and the drug trade.[34] These guerrillas have access to sufficient funds to purchase supplies on the black market. Lacking any sort of genuine international agenda, neither FARC nor the ELN require the type of diplomatic support that would clearly ally them with a state patron. As a result, the traditional

---

[31]"La Paz Sobre La Mesa," 1998.

[32]McNicholas, 2001.

[33]Ríos Rojas, Julian, "El Arsenal De Farc Y Eln," *El Espectador*, August 27, 2000.

[34]As mentioned earlier, FARC is much more heavily involved in the drug economy than is the ELN.

role of state sponsorship does not quite fit within the context of Colombia. However, if press reports are accurate, it would seem that sympathizers in Cuba and Venezuela have actively helped Colombia's guerrilla forces.[35]

CONCLUSION

Small-arms trafficking traditionally has not been a subject of extensive discussion with regard to U.S. interests in Colombia, much less in Latin America overall. Nonetheless, small-arms trafficking patterns *inform* the debate on the role of the U.S. government in Latin America and, more specifically, Colombia. As the United States conducts its war on terrorists who have global reach, FARC is increasingly being discussed. The following chapter, therefore, further explores patterns of arms trafficking to Colombia, with subsequent chapters providing a discussion of what these trafficking patterns mean for U.S. policy in the Latin American region.

---

[35]It is important to note that interviews the authors of this report conducted in the Latin American region also failed to produce any conclusive evidence of direct state sponsorship of guerrilla activity, but the interviews did point more definitely to at least some form of sympathetic support of that activity.

Chapter Three

PATTERNS OF SMALL-ARMS TRAFFICKING
INTO COLOMBIA

Small-arms trafficking patterns highlight the difficulties countries face when they attempt to control internal illegal markets fed by global trade. Although most people are aware that Colombia is a source of illegal drugs, it is simultaneously a repository for illegal small arms. The difference between the drug trade and weapons trafficking, however, is that Colombia is on the opposite side of the demand equation for weapons as compared with drugs. Colombia's arms trafficking patterns illuminate the dynamic of a strong central state confronted with political fighting perpetrated by insurgent forces and paramilitaries, while facing compound problems of violence, drugs, and the arms trafficking itself, all of which work together to continually weaken local authority.

GENERAL ARMS TRAFFICKING PATTERNS

Most small arms move from external sources into Colombia through black-market routes.[1] The arms trafficking data we gathered, covering the period from January 1998 to September 2001, revealed that 78 percent of the trafficking involves black-market activities.[2] Weapons

---

[1]The information in this chapter is derived from literally hundreds of sources. To eliminate the documentation difficulties associated with this number of sources, we cite only articles that include narratives on numerous routes, rather than cite every article that refers to a particular city, waterway, or method. For more information, see the appendix, which describes the methodology used to collect this information.

[2]See the appendix. (*Note:* References listed as "See the appendix" in this report indicate that the information was culled from or informed by the entire RAND data set, verified by author interviews, and not just from one or two specific sources.)

purchased in illegal markets are also transported via the "underground" and sold through Colombia's internal small-arms black market.

While it is tempting to assume that insurgents and drug dealers are responsible for purchasing all of the illegal weapons arriving in Colombia, this assumption is, in fact, incorrect. For example, for every private citizen who owns a registered firearm in Colombia at least three to four others possess an unregistered weapon.[3] And this estimate does not even include members of guerrilla or paramilitary organizations, only ordinary citizens. With such a high volume of small arms purchased illegally by a wide spectrum of Colombia's populace, it is difficult to isolate the weapons purchased and used exclusively by insurgents and even more difficult to ascertain the total volume of illegal arms sold and purchased in Colombia.

Moreover, these weapons are rarely trafficked or purchased in bulk (which would make tracing them easier). Instead, small arms "trickle" into Colombia by ones and twos or at most by the dozen, rather than cascading into the country by the thousands.

The plethora of trafficking venues underscores the vast dimensions of this market. There are 21 *known* arms trafficking routes from Venezuela, 26 from Ecuador, 37 from Panama, and 14 from Brazil.[4] Most of these routes involve small waterways through swamps or paths alongside the Amazon jungle or Darien Gap. Speedboats also regularly bring weapons into Colombia from coves along the Panamanian coast.

For example, Colombian authorities intercepted a small speedboat near the Pacific coast town of Juradó in January 1999.[5] The vessel was carrying 25 rifles, one machine gun, two submachine guns, one carbine, one rocket, several antitank grenades, and 40,000 rounds of

---

[3]Author interviews, Colombian security officials, Bogotá, June 2000; "El Tráfico De Armas En Bogotá," *El Espectador*, February 7, 2000.

[4]These numbers are those that have been historically provided by local authorities in the region. However, as Chapter Four outlines, our research revealed a number of additional routes.

[5]"Colombia: Navy Seizes Farc Weapons Coming from El Salvador," *Paris AFP*, January 4, 1999.

ammunition.[6] In another example, U.S. authorities arrested a man in Miami in December 2000 suspected of attempting to smuggle three machine guns, two semiautomatic pistols, a silencer, a flash suppressor, and six 30-round magazines into Colombia.[7]

Again, as isolated incidents go, these examples do not appear to be that significant. However, when viewed from a cumulative perspective, they are troublesome. One or two trucks smuggling a few guns across Colombia's border with Ecuador do not have strategic implications for the armed conflict in Colombia, but 5,000 trucks over the course of a year, each smuggling one or two guns, do. Indeed, an April 2001 investigative report estimated that some 10,000 small arms had been transported illegally across the border with Ecuador since 1999.[8] These incidents illustrate the second general trafficking pattern: Small arms constantly trickle into Colombia.

The third general trafficking pattern is that small arms are often cached. In February 2001, for example, the Colombian Armed Forces launched "Operation Black Cat" in the southwestern departments of Colombia. As part of this operation, the armed forces captured 560 rifles and 2,252 pistols in the Guainia Department alone.[9] However, discovering weapons that have been cached and, therefore, accumulated over an unknown period of time does not have the same policymaking implications as an interdiction of weapons. The Black Cat confiscation, for instance, did not tell the Colombian military how long the weapons had been in the Guainia Department nor how they got there. Moreover, the Colombian government did not know what effect such a seizure would have on FARC or the AUC without some knowledge of either group's overall stockpiles or immediate resource requirements. Similarly, the Black Cat confiscation did not provide information on how long ago the weapons had actually been pur-

---

[6]"Colombia: Navy Seizes Farc Weapons Coming from El Salvador," 1999.

[7]Tamayo, Juan, "Peru's Link to Arms Deal Worried U.S.," *Miami Herald*, September 20, 2000.

[8]Bedoya Lima, Jineth, "La Autopista De Las Farc En Plena Selva," *El Espectador*, April 27, 2001. Although the authors could not confirm this specific number, the basic pattern was validated through minutes of community meetings held along the border of Ecuador, which were obtained by the authors. Author interviews, Bogotá, April 2001.

[9]Martins, Marco Antonio, "Two of Beira-Mar's Girlfriends Still Evade Police," *Jornal do Brasil*, February 20, 2001.

chased, when and how they were transferred to the guerrillas or paramilitaries, or through which intermediaries they were transferred.

In a broader sense, the mere confiscation of weapons does not contribute to useful knowledge on the tactical sophistication of a group, its strategic plans or objectives, or its intentions. Nor can this information help policymakers make informed decisions based on these random seizures. Monitoring the flow of arms into a country, however, can reveal tactical adjustments made by a terrorist organization in direct response to military or police activities, and monitoring also sheds light on an organization's intentions or more-immediate aims and requirements.

Focusing on arms flows into Colombia, rather than focusing solely on individual caches, reveals an additional general trafficking pattern: FARC and the AUC are starting to buy in bulk. While most weapons are still entering Colombia singly or by the dozen, there have been a few recent reports of considerably larger shipments. These cases, however, may represent isolated exceptions to the rule. It is likely that FARC and the AUC are simply augmenting the normal "trickle" pattern as their operations, and therefore their demand, grow. For example, *Lima La Republica* reported that the authorities had intercepted an August 2000 communication between FARC and a Chinese contact in which FARC had asked for arms price quotes in both singles and thousands.[10] This communication suggests a deliberate change in FARC acquisition tactics and priorities, probably in response to a change in their perceived requirements. Similarly, in June 2000, reports circulated that the AUC was attempting to bring large shipments of AK-47s (totaling 4,000 weapons) into Barranco Minas on the border with Venezuela.[11] While these cases involve abnormally large shipments and, therefore, are possibly isolated instances, they nonetheless indicate that FARC and the AUC may be

---

[10]"Gunrunner Sarkis Links Peruvian Army, Sin to Arms Trafficking," *Lima La Republica*, September 21, 2000.

[11]See the appendix. Interestingly, some reports claim that the criminal working with the AUC then switched and sold these weapons to FARC. For example, see "Traición En El Mercado Negro De Armas," *El Tiempo*, June 28, 2000. Either way, the important point here is that the AUC was attempting to purchase in bulk.

struggling to arm their members and their new recruits quickly in preparation for stepped-up operations.

CENTRAL AMERICAN TRAFFICKING

Sources and Routes

Central America is an ideal location for funneling small arms into Colombia. Indeed, according to our research, five Central American countries—El Salvador, Honduras, Nicaragua, Panama, and to a lesser extent Costa Rica—account for some 36 percent of the total volume of small arms going into Colombia.[12] Past conflicts in Nicaragua, El Salvador, and Guatemala allowed the region to become a magnet for small arms in the 1980s and early 1990s. Although some of these weapons have been decommissioned, the percentage of weapons destroyed as compared with those remaining in Central America undoubtedly is very small.[13] For example, approximately 40,000 men (military and guerrillas) were demobilized at the end of El Salvador's civil war in 1992, and only slightly less than 9,000 small arms were destroyed (see Table 2.1 in Chapter Two). Thus, thousands of small arms likely are remaining in hidden caches across Central America.[14] Some observers argue that former left-wing guerrillas (e.g., former members of Frente Farabundo Martí para la Liberación Nacional [FMLN, El Salvador's Farabundo Marti National Liberation Front]) provide these cached weapons to FARC for

---

[12]See the appendix.

[13]In fact, one of the problems with using the euphemistic term "decommissioning" is a lack of precision in the literature we reviewed for this study about whether the term refers to the actual destruction of weapons, their mere surrender, or their stockpiling (in possibly vulnerable repositories). The distinction is by no means academic: In some instances, "decommissioned" weapons find their way back into the hands of criminals, terrorists, guerrillas, or ordinary citizens.

[14]Boutwell, Jeffrey, and Michael Klare, eds., *Light Weapons and Civil Conflict: Controlling the Tools of Violence*, New York: Rowman & Littlefield, 1999, p. 187. Laurance and Godnick (Laurance, Edward, and William Godnick, "Weapons Collection in Central America: El Salvador and Guatemala," in *Managing the Remnants of War: Weapons Collection and Disposal as an Element of Peace-Building*, Bonn, Germany: Bonn International Center for Conversion, 2000) estimated that more than 200,000 small arms remained in El Salvador after the 1992 peace accords.

political reasons.[15] While there are definite reasons to believe that former guerrillas remain sympathetic to the left-wing FARC and ELN, more likely the vendors are unscrupulous entrepreneurs who acquire and sell to paramilitaries and guerrillas alike, depending on the highest bidder.

In addition to being a source for small arms, Central America is also an important arms transit route. Currently, Panama is the *single largest transit route* for small arms flowing into Colombia; the Darien Gap, which lies along the border with Colombia, acts as the main collection and dissemination point. The terrain is densely forested, making it ideal for gathering and smuggling small amounts of weapons into Colombia's Chocó Department via ground routes. The Darien Gap also contains a number of small coves that maritime traffickers use to access Colombia's Caribbean and Pacific coasts by sea. These transit routes not only make it difficult for the Colombian government to control small-arms flows, they also directly impact the internal security of the transit state. Therefore, the relationship between Central American countries as the supply side and Colombia as the demand side contributes appreciably to the downward spiral of Colombia's deteriorating security, in addition to undermining governmental authority throughout the entire region.

Small-Arms Collection and Distribution

Cities and ports in El Salvador, Honduras, Nicaragua, Panama, and Costa Rica form a chain of small-arms collection points and distribution routes. This system is sophisticated, abetted by weak and corrupt local officials, the forested terrain, and easy access to weapons stocks. International gray-market[16] traffickers, including the Russian mafia, Chinese Triads, agents for the Euskadi ta Askatasuna (ETA) (Basque separatist terrorist group), Yasir Arafat's al Fatah, and

---

[15]"Mala Ventura," *Semana,* September 11, 2000.

[16]Small arms are purchased in three different markets: *white, gray,* and *black*. White markets for military weapons include weapons bought and sold by authorized private manufacturers or state-owned enterprises. Gray markets occupy the space between white-market activities and the illegal trade in small arms. In the gray market, a state may arrange for an arms transfer to an illegitimate actor for political or economic purposes, but conceal the transfer in legal channels. Black-market activities are completely illegal. These markets are more fully discussed in Chapter Five.

Lebanon's Hezbollah, also utilize this system.[17] Our focus here, though, is on black-market routes within Central America, which specifically feed into Colombia's conflict.

El Salvador, Honduras, and Nicaragua serve primarily as source countries, rather than as transit routes. Their designation as "source countries" does not mean that their local companies produce small arms for the black market, nor does it mean that all of the weapons from these three countries come from old caches. Some munitions trickle into Nicaragua and Honduras from the Caribbean, the United States, and Mexico. Weapons coming from El Salvador mostly cross into Nicaragua and Honduras first, and then continue on to Colombia. El Salvador, Honduras, and Nicaragua together, therefore, serve as the first link in a chain of trafficking routes that bring weapons into Colombia. They are collection points and distribution hubs from which the weapons are gathered together in small clusters and then delivered into the black market.

There are three primary collection hubs in Honduras and Nicaragua:

The first hub is Catacamas, Honduras.[18] Weapons are gathered together in small collections as they come into Catacamas by river and ground routes. They are then transported over land to the Rio Sico, traveling northeast until they arrive at Cabo Camerón on the Caribbean coast of Honduras.

The second hub is Estelí, Nicaragua. Weapons collected at Estelí are transported by land to the Rio Patuca, across the border in Honduras.[19] The Rio Patuca also flows northeast, joining with the Caribbean at Barra Patuca, Honduras. Weapons from both Cabo Camerón and Barra Patuca then travel down the Caribbean and Pacific coasts to San Andrés Island, to ports along Panama's eastern coast, or even directly to northeastern Colombia.[20]

---

[17]"Mercado Blanco De Armas," *Cambio*, March 1, 1999.

[18]"Los Misiles De Las Farc," *Semana*, September 6, 1999, p. 22.

[19]"Los Misiles De Las Farc," 1999, p. 22.

[20]For a discussion of San Andrés Island, see "Colombia, Un 'San Andresito' De Armamento," *El País*, August 22, 2000, p. 2; Lunazzi, Eduardo, "San Andres Se Pone En Guardia," *El Tiempo*, October 16, 1994. p. 21A; Lunazzi, Eduardo, "San Andres, Puente

The third collection hub is Managua, Nicaragua.[21] The geography of Managua is perfect for smuggling because it provides access to both land and water routes. Weapons travel from Managua to Punta Perlas or to Bluefields (Nicaragua), utilizing the Pan-American Highway as well as water routes.[22] From either of these two points, traffickers ship the weapons to San Andrés Island via Corn Island and then to the northeast coast of Colombia.[23] Alternatively, arms can be transported to Guabito (Panama) and then to Caracas or ports on Colombia's Caribbean seaboard.[24]

In addition to the collection points and trafficking routes in Honduras and Nicaragua, there are three major points and routes in Costa Rica and El Salvador:

The first conduit begins with three rivers (Rio Frio, Rio Zapote, and Rio San Carlos) that allow smugglers to gather weapons in Los Chiles on the border between Costa Rica and Nicaragua.[25] These weapons are then transported along the border between these two countries on the San Juan River to San Juan del Norte. Like Cabo Camarón and Barra Patuca, San Juan del Norte is a "hub" port that allows weapons to be transferred onto water vessels and over to San Andrés Island, Providencia Island, Corn Island, or even to Panama.[26]

The second route begins with its collection point in Armuelles, Panama. Armuelles is in the northwestern-most part of Panama. But rather than working their way down Panama's Pacific coastline, these weapons cross into Costa Rica by land and travel to the Isla

---

De Armas Y Narcotrafico Dice Mindefensa," *El Tiempo*, October 15, 1994, p. 7A; and "San Andres, Un Paraiso Artificial," *El Tiempo*, October 17, 1994b.

[21]"Los Misiles De Las Farc," 1999; McNicholas, Michael, *Colombian Guerrilla and Para-Military Arms Procurement: Origin and Routes*, Panama City: Phoenix Group, 2001.

[22]"Los Misiles De Las Farc," 1999; McNicholas, 2001; "San Andres: Un Paraiso Artificial," 1994a.

[23]"San Andres: Un Paraiso Artificial," 1994a.

[24]"La Muerte Al Menudeo," *Semana*, May 3, 1999, pp. 40–47; "Los Misiles De Las Farc," 1999; McNicholas, 2001.

[25]"Los Misiles De Las Farc," 1999.

[26]"El Sur, 'Paraíso' De Traficantes De La Guerra," *El País*, May 7, 2000; "Los Misiles De Las Farc," 1999.

Bastimentos. From there, the weapons travel by sea to Colón or to Puerto Obaldia on Panama's Caribbean coast.[27]

The final route begins in Santa Ana, El Salvador. From there, the weapons are transshipped over land to Acajutla and then south on the Pan-American Highway to Panama.[28] Weapons from El Salvador are also sometimes transferred onto small coastal freighters or fishing vessels that travel south along the western seaboard of Central America until they reach Balboa, Panama. Small ports along this route, including Punta Chame, San Carlos, Rio Hato, Pedasi, or Puerto Mutis, are also used as stop-off points for weapons that travel from Panama to Colombia's Pacific ports.[29]

Panama has two roles with respect to arms trafficking and Colombia. It is a Central American source for illicit weapons, but it also borders Colombia along the Darien Gap and therefore acts as an important transit state (this topic is examined later in the "Arms Flowing from Neighboring Countries" section). In terms of acting as a source for small arms, Colón represents the main Panamanian hub. Weapons that originate in Colón appear to come from criminal and insurgent groups—e.g., Chinese Triads or ETA. Some of these munitions cross the Panama Canal into Panama City and are then moved overland through Chepo, eventually arriving on FARC bases in southern Panama. Others are transferred to the Isla del Rey in the Gulf of Panama and then smuggled south via the Darien Gap or Colombia's Pacific ports.[30]

There is very little detailed information available that links transportation methods to the specific routes discussed in this report. But some informed assumptions can be made based on the general terrain of the routes, types of ports, and destination cities. For example, the Brazilian military has tracked arms trafficking shipments via shallow-water motorboats up the Rio Icana to Mitú in Colombia.[31] It

---

[27]"Mercado Blanco De Armas," 1999, p. 44.

[28]McNicholas, 2001.

[29]McNicholas, 2001.

[30]"Mercado Blanco De Armas," 1999, p. 44.

[31]Franco, Ilimar, "Pf to Block Farc Supply Routes in Amazon," *Jornal do Brasil*, August 20, 1999.

is reasonable to posit that smugglers in Central America implement similar methods when transporting weapons up the Rio Sico and Rio Patuca. In addition, small fishing vessels often bring arms from Panama to the coasts of Colombia, and it is likely that other smugglers follow the same basic pattern from locations farther north in Central America.[32] So, rather than large cargo ships, it is probable that small fishing vessels and maritime craft are used to bring small arms from Honduras and Nicaragua to ports on San Andrés Island or on Panama's coastline.

When shipping weapons over land, traffickers in Colombia have attempted to hide weapons and ammunition among produce, such as potatoes or cereal, as it is being transported to town markets for sale.[33] In the tri-borders area (Argentina, Brazil, and Paraguay), illegal commodities are also hidden among tourist goods.[34] Again, a similar method is probably used by those transporting small arms on roadways inside Nicaragua or Honduras.

The significance of the arms trafficking patterns discussed here (i.e., the routes and methods) is that they lend themselves more easily to black-market trade than to large-scale gray-market smuggling. If weapons are collected and transported through small towns and ports by small fishing vessels or smuggled individually in trucks, middlemen do not require forged end-user certificates, sophisticated coverups, or any of the other illegal methods typically used by state-sponsored smugglers or criminal groups. As a result, interdicting trafficking patterns to Colombia requires more-active, targeted, systematic, and strategic policy than the general international monitoring regulations or enforcement of those regulations. Monitoring huge shipments or tightening regulations on end-user certificates might eliminate some of the general trafficking activity, but an effective policy must also address smaller smuggling efforts and the overall black-market trade.

---

[32]"Traición En El Mercado Negro De Armas," 2000, pp. 1–11.

[33]Simancas, Javier, "Ecuador, 'Santuario' Del Tráfico De Armas," *El País*, July 16, 2000; Wood, Brian, and Johan Peleman, *The Arms Fixers: Controlling Brokers and Shipping Agents*, Oslo: Norwegian Initiative on Small Arms Transfers, 1999, Chapters 4–5.

[34]"Four Days in the City of Terror," *Ma'ariv*, October 7, 1994, pp. 2–5.

Summary

The sources and transit routes described in this chapter do not provide a complete picture of all arms trafficking patterns from Central America. But they do clearly illustrate how arms are collected in Central America for distribution into Colombia. The arms trade in Central America is conducted in black markets. None of the weapons trafficking incidents that we studied indicates any significant gray- or white-market trade from Central America to Colombia's insurgents. This observation is fairly logical. In recent years, Central American countries have not exported or imported a high volume of guns. It would therefore be difficult to conceal gray-market transfers to these countries. In addition, such weapons are easily available from Cold War–era caches, making it simple to obtain weapons in a total black market.

A more striking pattern that emerges from our analysis is that weapons enter Colombia from El Salvador, Honduras, Nicaragua, and Costa Rica mostly via sea routes. At the same time, however, small-arms trafficking is by no means *isolated* to sea routes: Small arms enter Colombia via ground routes and river routes as well.[35] As mentioned previously, this pattern is not entirely identical to the arms trafficking patterns found in Panama, which also borders Colombia. These frontier countries display slightly different arms trafficking patterns, focusing more on land and air routes. The next section examines how small arms get into Colombia from Venezuela, Brazil, Peru, Ecuador, and Panama.

ARMS FLOWING FROM NEIGHBORING COUNTRIES

One of the main challenges that countries such as Colombia face when dealing with arms trafficking is border control, and one of their main concerns is the degree of help with border control they can expect to receive from neighbors. Each of the countries bordering Colombia has a discrete set of geopolitical characteristics that contribute to the flow of arms into Colombia's arms market. Venezuela's northwestern border provides traffickers with close access to the Caribbean through the Gulf of Venezuela, while its southwestern

---

[35]See the appendix.

border is composed of easily penetrated marshes. The sparsely populated Amazon jungle forms a natural border along Brazil's northwest frontier. The Panamanian, Peruvian, and Ecuadorian borders are equally rugged and therefore are difficult to monitor. As a result, Colombia has been forced to rely on the combined efforts of its own military, police, and customs forces along with those of other governments to secure its frontiers. This interaction proves to be problematic when it involves monitoring the flow of smaller commodities that are easy to conceal, such as guns.

Like the countries in Central America, Colombia's neighbors in South America also act as sources of small arms as well as transit routes. Yet, there is a crucial difference between Central America and Colombia's neighbors as sources of illegal weapons: Colombia's neighbors do not have the same available arms caches that Central American countries have. As a result, traffickers typically purchase weapons from criminal organizations, obtain them from internal legal markets, bribe private security forces to obtain them, or raid government military stockpiles. Because weapons from Colombia's neighbors come from such disparate sources, it is difficult to identify specific arms trafficking patterns and routes in those neighboring countries. This variety of means and methods (much less origins) also makes it much less likely that a single interdiction will have a significant impact on the flow of arms into Colombia. The more dispersed a distribution network, the less traffickers rely on any one route, and the less impact interdiction efforts directed to any one route will have on overall trafficking patterns.

Neighboring Countries' Sources

Weapons routinely move from Venezuela into Colombia. Some of those arms are registered to the Venezuelan Armed Forces, while others are black-market items that have circuitously traveled from Mexico, Israel, Brazil, and Spain.[36] As of this writing, there are no definitive documents in the public domain that link the Venezuelan state with Colombia's guerrillas or paramilitaries.

---

[36]"Authorities Seize Ammunition Shipment in Border Area," *El Nacional*, September 29, 2000; Simancas, 2000.

Rumors have repeatedly surfaced, however, that members of Venezuela's armed forces who are sympathetic to FARC and the ELN have supplied the groups with weapons and ammunition. Three main reports account for these allegations. First, Colombian security forces have discovered several illegal caches of weapons (totaling approximately 400 rifles) that have been linked back to Venezuela's Compania Anonima Benezolana Industrial de Municiones.[37] Second, in July 1999, Colombian authorities arrested Josue Eliseo Prieto (a.k.a. Esteban), the head of FARC finances, while he was meeting with four Venezuelan citizens. Colombian authorities subsequently found documents indicating that FARC had met with members of the Judicial Technical Police of Venezuela.[38] Finally, a guerrilla captured by the AUC told members of the group that the Venezuelan Army was supplying the ELN with small arms and training.[39] These three reports have yet to be definitively confirmed, but they still remain a source of serious concern.

Brazil is another a source of illegal weapons. Iguazu Falls is a significant source of illicit goods for the entire region, including Colombia. The area is part of the tri-border black market, which links Argentina, Paraguay, and Brazil. FARC agents reportedly operate both in Iguazu Falls and along Brazil's border with Paraguay. Although reports of FARC activities in this region do not elaborate on the specific activities of FARC agents, the area is well known as a source for drugs, weapons, and money laundering.[40]

In December 2000, Colombian authorities arrested FARC member Ricardo Marquez Patino in Leticia.[41] Tabatinga (Brazil) and Leticia (Colombia) form a pivot point for black-market activity in general, and arms trafficking in particular. These examples suggest that FARC is actively inserting purchasing agents in the regions' various illegal arms markets.

---

[37]Ríos Rojas, Julian, "El Arsenal De Farc Y Eln," *El Espectador*, August 27, 2000, p. 2.

[38]"General Tapias on Puerto Lleras Attack," *Semana*, July 11, 1999.

[39]"Militares Venezolanos Entrenaron Al Eln," *El Tiempo*, March 29, 2001.

[40]Author interviews, Argentina, January 2000, and Bogotá, June 2000.

[41]"Army Reports Heavy Child Involvement in Guerrilla War," *El País*, December 27, 2000.

FARC has also raided Brazilian Federal Police posts in the Amazon region, stealing weapons, ammunition, and medical supplies.[42] The group asserts that such "raids" are a primary source of weapons for their organization.[43] This claim, however, is dubious: When FARC raided the stocks of the Ecuadorian Montufar battalion in July 2000, the raid netted FARC only 48 rifles and 68 charges.[44] It should also be pointed out that FARC devotes a considerable amount of its financial resources to arms procurement, spending approximately $2,000 per year for each fighting member of the organization.[45] This amount includes salaries for the group's leaders and weapons and supplies costs, but excludes salaries for ordinary members of guerrilla units.[46] The AUC spends approximately $1,500 per person per year on war materials alone.[47] To place these numbers in perspective, local Colombian newspapers report black-market prices for an AK-47 in Colombia ranging from $900 to $3,500.[48] Although FARC and the AUC do not have to purchase weapons for its fighters annually, these numbers do indicate that both groups (especially the AUC) are nonetheless spending a considerable amount of money for weapons and ammunition each year. If they were stealing the majority of these weapons, expenditure levels would be significantly lower. These figures, therefore, suggest that FARC and the AUC are purchasing weapons more frequently than they are stealing them.

Both FARC and the AUC need a constant supply of weapons for new members and operations. The increase in fighting between these or-

---

[42]"Brazil Police Assess Notes on Weapons-for-Drugs Scheme Headed by Beira-Mar," *Zero Hora*, March 15, 2001; Ferraz, Silvio, "Armed Forces Mobilize in Response to Farc," *Sao Paulo Veja*, November 10, 1999.

[43]"Arms Trafficking to Colombia Increases," *El Comercio*, August 23, 2000.

[44]Simancas, 2000.

[45]"Los Costos Del Cese Al Fuego," *El País*, July 6, 2000, p. 1.

[46]McDermott, Jeremy, "Welcome to Farclandia," *BBC News*, Internet edition, January 13, 2001 (available from http://news.bbc.co.uk; last accessed July 17, 2001).

[47]"Las Finanzas De Los Paras," *Cambio*, May 15, 2000, p. 14.

[48]Individuals interviewed in Colombia believed that these figures were too high. Yet, the authors could not confirm any lower prices. Needless to say, the prices for weapons in the black market fluctuate dramatically. The range of costs was cited in the following articles: "La Muerte Al Menudeo," 1999; "Los Costos Del Cese Al Fuego," 2000; "Traición En El Mercado Negro De Armas," 2000, pp. 1–11; and "Mercado Negro A Pesar Del Desarme," *El Tiempo*, August 2, 1999.

ganizations has forced both groups to recruit new members from lo-cal women and children as well as from their usual constituency.[49] FARC, in particular, has appeared to be having some initial difficulty arming these new recruits. For example, some FARC members who have been captured by the Colombian National Police or who have turned themselves in were in possession of little more than a few grenades.[50] In addition, FARC has issued statements against the crop eradication programs in Putamayo, claiming that it is arming and training local residents for self-defense,[51] yet the group allows these trainees to shoot only one or two rounds, and then takes away the guns after the "training" is completed.[52] But military stockpiles could provide FARC (or the AUC) with more extensive supplies at critical moments, creating a strong incentive for cross-border raids into neighboring countries. Although Brazil has increased its border con-trol and surveillance,[53] its frontier is dense and sparsely populated with many small water and ground routes into Colombia's Amazonas, Vaupes, and Guainia Departments; any measure of in-creased control gained by Brasilia is therefore likely to be limited at best.

Colombian military forces have also confiscated small arms pro-duced in both Peru and Ecuador. But like patterns of arms trafficking from Central America, a trickle of weapons can have a significant cumulative impact on Colombia if it is constant and unrelenting.

Significant arms flows have, finally, been traced back to Ecuador.[54] Military authorities have periodically reported the loss of weapons to

---

[49]Penhaul, Karl, "Colombia's Communist Guerrillas Take on Feminine Face," *Boston Globe*, Internet edition, January 7, 2001 (available from www.boston.com; last ac-cessed January 9, 2001); Wilson, Scott, "Colombia's Other Army," *Washington Post*, March 12, 2001a.

[50]"Army Reports Heavy Child Involvement in Guerrilla War," 2000.

[51]In 2000, for instance, FARC specifically asserted that it has the "task and responsibil-ity of organizing the people so that they can defend themselves against aggressors, even more so if a foreign state [U.S.] intervenes to fight against drug traffickers" ("El Otro Plan Colombia," *Cambio*, March 20, 2000, p. 24).

[52]Author interview, journalist, Bogotá, April 2001.

[53]Franco, 1999.

[54]Apart from being a source of weapons, Ecuador also represents a source of black-market fuel for Colombia, much of which originates from the Sucumbios region (Mauricio Vega, Carlos, "La Caldera Del Diablo," *Cambio*, November 20, 2000, p. 54).

Colombian insurgents. In July 2000, for instance, Ecuadorian General Narvaez told reporters that 48 rifles had been taken from an Ecuadorian military storehouse near Esmeraldas.[55] At least 22 private security forces have also been accused of reselling legal arms on the black market, many of which are believed to have ended up in the hands of groups fighting in Colombia.[56] Ordinary citizens represent an additional source of weapons. Increases in cross-border violence have prompted many Ecuadorians to buy guns for personal protection, some of which have been sold to guerrillas for profit or used as part of kidnapping ransoms.[57]

These last two patterns—arms flows from Ecuador and average citizens as a source of weapons—illustrate the dynamic relationship between legal and illegal arms sales in the region. Licit stocks of military weapons are either looted by insurgents or injected illegally into the black market. The same pattern exists with legal personal weapons that are sold to insurgent groups by individuals for a profit. While these white-market stocks (at origin) do not constitute the total amount of small arms in the black market, they do contribute to the complexity of the relationship between legal and illegal arms sales.

Neighboring Countries' Land Routes

The most significant roles that Colombia's neighbors play in arms trafficking, however, are as transshipment and transit points. Land routes pose a particular policy problem because most weapons that travel along these conduits are in small quantities. This situation has detracted from land routes' perceived importance (as arms routes), encouraging policymakers to focus on eliminating higher-volume sea- or air-route supplies instead. However, land routes provide guerrillas with their most constant supply of small arms and, as such, are of major strategic importance for the operational capabilities of FARC, the ELN in particular, and to a lesser extent the AUC.

---

[55]Simancas, 2000.

[56]"Colombia, En La Mira," *El Tiempo*, June 28, 2001 (electronic archives; last accessed July 5, 2001).

[57]Author interview, Bogotá, April 2001; "Farc Retains Cars, Demands Ransom in Northwestern Colombia," *Paris AFP*, December 28, 2000.

In addition to acting as a source of arms, Venezuela also provides transit routes for weapons that come through the country on their way to Colombia. Most of these conduits are land based. Weapons typically arrive into the port of Paraguaipoa on the Gulf of Venezuela where they are transferred to ground vehicles and brought into Maicao (Colombia) and down to Villanueva for distribution into the rest of Colombia.[58] The Gulf of Venezuela is situated in the northwestern part of the country, allowing traffickers easy access to Colombia's borders and to a major north-south highway. This route forms a significant ELN supply chain.

Arms also cross from Venezuela into Tibú in Colombia's Norte de Santander Department. From there, the weapons travel down a main road to Convención and Ocaña.[59] A significant portion of this route passes along border swampland, making the entry points fairly amorphous (a problem that is particularly acute in Venezuela's Táchira Department). From any given point along the frontier between the two countries, for example at Venezuela's Ureña, arms flow into Cúcuta, Colombia, and then travel down a major highway to Bucaramanga and eventually arrive in Barrancabermeja.[60]

Weapons also enter into Colombia along its land border with Ecuador. As with Venezuela, these routes follow major regional highways. One particularly heavily used conduit is the roadway that FARC built from the Ecuadorian border to Colombia's Putamayo Department. An estimated 10,000 small arms have arrived into Colombia from along this route since 1998.[61] Weapons also move

---

[58]"La Muerte Al Menudeo," 1999, p. 44.

[59]"La Muerte Al Menudeo," 1999, p. 44.

[60]Barrancabermeja is significant because it is the headquarters of the oil company Ecopetrol. As such, it has been a central point of contention between the ELN (which has attacked oil interests) and the AUC. For example, in May 2001, Colombian authorities discovered two cars filled with explosives in Barrancabermeja. The authorities suspect that these bombs were planted as part of an ongoing struggle between the ELN and the AUC to gain control over the city. Furthermore, Barrancabermeja's neighboring city, Bucaramanga, is a logistical hub for northeastern Colombia. It links three major highways and works as an internal distribution route for both the ELN and the AUC. Because of this strategic transportation route, the Colombian Department Norte de Santander, and its capital city Barrancabermeja in particular, are focal points of urban warfare between the AUC and the ELN ("Desactivan Dos Carros Bomba En Barrancabermeja," El Tiempo, May 25, 2001).

[61]Bedoya Lima, 2001.

from Nuevo Loja (Ecuador) to Oríto and Puerto Asís (Colombia).[62] These arms are eventually transported through El Tablón and La Cruz, probably destined for FARC's demilitarized zone. Small arms also enter through Ecuador's Tulcán to Ipiales and finally via a major highway north into Pasto (Colombia) for distribution either to Cali or FARC's DMZ.[63] Another important route begins in the port city Esmeraldas (Ecuador), traveling east overland to Turfiño and then north to Chiles (Colombia). This arms conduit feeds both the DMZ and the fighting in Colombia's Nariño Department; it is particularly interesting that the conduit uses neither FARC's DMZ nor a major city as a distribution point but rather feeds directly into the conflict in Nariño. This distinction could be random, or it could indicate a deliberate move toward decentralization of FARC's decisionmaking structure.

Traffickers also use land routes to transport weapons from Panama. Panama was discussed earlier in this chapter in relation to Central America, but its border with Colombia is also a serious source of contention between the AUC and FARC. FARC has established bases in Panama's Darien Gap, and the AUC has been moving agents into the region as it increases its own participation in the drug economy. Furthermore, both FARC and the AUC have been using ports along Panama's eastern seaboard to bring weapons into Colombia. FARC, in particular, concentrates on the Gulf of Urabá (although the FARC and AUC have been fighting for control of the Chocó and Córdoba Departments since 1994),[64] while the AUC adopts a broader approach, using several ports to bring weapons into Santa Marta, Turbo, Riohacha, and Portete.[65]

Since the spring of 2001, the AUC, FARC, and the ELN have been targeting Colombia's Chocó and Antioquia Departments. The significance of this activity is that these groups are not just fighting for control of the border area but also for the sake of expansion. Chocó and Antioquia have strategic value: The group that controls these departments controls access to Panama's land and sea distribution

---

[62]"Arms Trafficking to Colombia Increases," 2000; Simancas, 2000.

[63]"Panamá, Ruta Preferida Por Traficantes," *El Espectador*, September 10, 2000.

[64]"Informe Especial: La Tierra Del Olvido," *Semana*, June 15, 1998, p. 51.

[65]McNicholas, 2001.

routes. In April 2000, Panamanian authorities claimed that they knew of almost 200 paths in the Darien Gap used by traffickers.[66] This number of pathways illustrates the enormity of the trafficking problem along Colombia's border with Panama.

Panama poses a particular problem for controlling weapons flows because dividing its arms trafficking patterns among land, air, or sea is difficult. This difficulty arises largely because FARC has bases in the Darien Gap that operate as logistical hubs for purchasing and delivering arms. These operational bases allow FARC to control routes and move weapons back and forth between land, sea, and air.

Chapter Four discusses in detail land routes for the shipment of weapons from Panama to Colombia. However, a few additional conduits within Panama's southern provinces merit further discussion here. Distribution hubs such as Coquira (Chepo) and Quimbo (La Palma) allow traffickers to move weapons from boats onto vehicles and from vehicles onto boats. When transported by land, arms from Coquira or Quimbo travel south to Meteti where they are placed on small riverboats, which eventually transport the weapons to a FARC base west of Cerro Bell.[67] Weapons are placed onto riverboats in Quimbo, which transport the arms down the Tuira and Pirre Rivers to FARC units operating in the northern Serrania de Pierre Mountains.[68] These land routes (within Panama) combine with the maritime trafficking from other Central American countries (into Panama), making Panama the single largest route for arms trafficking into Colombia.

Finally, smugglers utilize the dense Amazon along Colombia's border with Brazil to transport weapons into the country via ground routes. Rather than using vehicles, these weapons are brought in from Brazil via river craft.[69] Small motorboats bring weapons from Manaus (Brazil) up the Rio Negro to San Joaquin and then continue up the

---

[66]Delgado, Naya, "Panama Becomes Bazaar for Central American Weapons," *Reuters*, Internet edition, April 21, 2000 (last accessed September 25, 2000).

[67]McNicholas, 2001.

[68]McNicholas, 2001.

[69]Rivers are considered "land" routes versus sea routes in this report, primarily because the geographic characteristics and logistical requirements for river route smuggling are more similar to land route smuggling than sea route smuggling.

Rio Icana and the Rio Uaupés to Mitú, Colombia.[70] Although it is difficult to directly link the smuggling of arms across Brazil's border to one insurgent group, previous fighting plus proximity to the DMZ indicate that the Brazilian-Colombian border is primarily a FARC trafficking route.[71]

Neighboring Countries' Sea and Air Routes

Weapons shipments that come into Colombia by sea and air are grouped together in larger bundles than those that are transported by surface routes. For example, a shipment of 25 AK-47s might be brought in by sea as opposed to 2 AK-47s smuggled in over land. It should be noted, however, that illegal arms traffickers use mostly small charter planes to bring weapons into Colombia, which does limit the number of weapons that can be transported at one time. There are a few exceptions to this general rule, which are discussed in the next section "Larger Shipments of Arms."

Arms traffickers use small fishing vessels to transport weapons directly into a Pacific or Caribbean port. They also pack the weapons in plastic bags and drop them into the sea, and then wait for the arms to be dragged to shore by even smaller boats.[72] Arms flowing to FARC typically arrive via the Pacific seaboard, while those going to the AUC are trafficked through the Caribbean port of Santa Marta and through smaller hubs around the Gulf of Morrosquillo and the Cordoba Department.[73] This pattern reflects division of maritime control, which at the time of this writing remained in force.[74] It should be noted, however, that in September 2000, AUC leader Carlos Castaño told a reporter from Bogotá's *El Tiempo*, "We are be-

---

[70]"Brazil's 'Pablo Escobar' Exchanged Arms for Drugs with Farc," *El Espectador*, February 20, 2001; Ferraz, 1999.

[71]Mitú has been a frequent site of fighting between FARC and the Colombian military. In 1997 and 1998, FARC defeated the Colombian military in Las Delicias, Puerres, el Billar, Miraflores, and Mitú. FARC launched another series of attacks against Mitú in the winter of 1999. FARC specifically targeted military posts to obtain medical and ammunition supplies.

[72]"Traición En El Mercado Negro De Armas," 2000.

[73]"Panamá, Ruta Preferida Por Traficantes," 2000.

[74]The exception to this general pattern is FARC's use of the Gulf of Urabá (as mentioned previously) and the AUC's access to Bahai Solano (McNicholas, 2001).

coming involved in the Pacific to eradicate Front 30 of the FARC."[75] Since that interview with Castaño, fighting between guerrillas and paramilitaries has steadily increased, indicating that even FARC's traditional stronghold of Buenaventura is under contention.[76]

Ecuador provides access to Colombia's internal market from both land and sea routes. In July 2000, Ecuadorian authorities confiscated approximately 6,000 rounds of 7.62-caliber ammunition, intended to be transported to Colombia by sea. The authorities suspected that this ammunition was related to a cache of rifles discovered by Colombian security forces and attributed to FARC. Ammunition and weapons generally leave Esmeraldas (Ecuador) and are then deposited in Tumaco and in Buenaventura, which has historically served as a hub for drugs and weapons trafficking.[77] It is likely that these routes are used primarily by FARC. Of all the insurgents, FARC has the strongest presence in the southwestern departments of Colombia. But FARC's 2001 movement into Nariño is fairly new. It appears that FARC made a strategic decision to move out of the area dominated by the AUC and to secure its access to supplies through the Pacific coast instead.

Approximately 50 percent of illegal weapons shipments entering Colombia by sea come in from Panama.[78] Panama's coastline is such that weapons could conceivably leave from any number of small coves. Accordingly, it is difficult to identify with any degree of accuracy the entire scope of illicit Panamanian-Colombian maritime traffic. However, the available data indicate that there are two primary points of departure traffickers use for access to Colombia's Pacific coast—Panama City or Isla del Rey. From there, weapons are transferred to Jurado, Cupica Bay, Gulf of Tibuga, Bahai Solano, or Buenaventura.[79] Illegal arms traffickers also bring weapons directly into Colombia via Caribbean ports, using either Puerto Obaldia (Panama) or San Andrés Island (Colombia) to ship weapons into

---

[75]"Colombia, En La Mira," 2001.

[76]"Mala Ventura," 2000.

[77]Simancas, 2000.

[78]See the appendix.

[79]"Incautadas Quince Mil Armas En Cinco Años," *El País,* July 11, 2000; McNicholas, 2001.

Acandí, Tolú (Gulf of Morrosquillo), or Santa Marta.[80] The AUC controls these ports.

Panama also acts as a minor base for illegal arms trafficking flights to Colombia. Planes fly from Panama into El Banco, Magdalena, or Acandí, Chocó.[81] Weapons are then transferred to vehicles and distributed overland (for a discussion on routes inside Colombia, see Chapter Four).

Our research indicated that slightly less than half of all illegal arms shipments that arrive in Colombia via air routes depart from Brazil. These weapons are flown from Brazil or Suriname into small airfields in FARC's demilitarized zone or in the Guainia or Vichada Departments.[82] The widely publicized activities of gun trafficker Luiz Fernando da Costa (a.k.a. Ferandinho Beira-Mar) are indicative of movements that take place along this route. The "Beira-Mar" traffickers delivered a total of 2,400 handguns and 543 rifles to Barranco Minas, Colombia, during three months of spring 2001.[83] In 2000, Colombian authorities intercepted approximately 45 flights from Brazil, Paraguay, and Suriname that they linked directly to arms trafficking.[84] Like the planes flying from Panama, these small single-engine charter planes carry approximately 1,000 to 2,000 pounds of cargo. In terms of weapons, this would equate to about 100 AK-47s, not including ammunition.

It is difficult to distinguish between illegal air traffic for drug trafficking and illegal air traffic for weapons trafficking. For example, a plane might arrive at a destination with weapons and leave with drugs, as is suspected in the case of Beira-Mar. This logistical link between illegal drug trafficking routes and arms trafficking routes is a distinct char-

---

[80]"Das Seizes Smuggled Nicaraguan Military Rifles," 2000a; "Panamá, Ruta Preferida Por Traficantes," 2000.

[81]"Colombia, Un "San Andresito" De Armamento," 2000; "Panamá, Ruta Preferida Por Traficantes," 2000.

[82]"Colombia, En La Mira," 2001; Rocio Vasquez, Claudia, "42 Vuelos De Trafico De Armas," *El Tiempo*, August 27, 2000, p. 3.

[83]"Brazil Police Assess Notes on Weapons-for-Drugs Scheme Headed by Beira-Mar," 2001.

[84]"Authorities Seize Jordanian Arsenal Shipped to Farc," Bogotá: Caracol Colombia Radio, reprint, FBIS-LAT-2000-1216, 2000; Rocio Vasquez, 2000.

acteristic of air trafficking patterns that has two possible explanations. First, an air shipment simply costs more than a land shipment. A pilot and his crew might get paid between $5,000 and $30,000 plus the cost of renting the aircraft.[85] Therefore, there is an incentive for traffickers to make as much money as possible during both legs of the trip. Second, bringing weapons in by air requires a higher level of sophistication. Pilots have to avoid commercial routes and air space monitored by traffic controllers, land on rough airstrips, and even parachute drop cargo over a specific location.[86] As a result, if any trafficking patterns lean toward association with transnational criminal organizations, it is those that rely on air routes given the higher degree of sophistication that use of those routes requires.

LARGER SHIPMENTS OF ARMS

The general pattern of arms trafficking in Colombia has seen an increase in the number of shipments since 1999, although not necessarily a rise in volume per shipment. Two separate incidents of larger shipments may indicate a shift by FARC and the AUC toward buying in bulk.

First, from March until August 1999, the Jordanian government sold 10,000 AK-47s to the Peruvian Army and National Intelligence Services. These weapons were air dropped from three separate cargo planes in March, April, and July 1999 as they flew over Colombia.[87] This transfer took place in the gray market. The arms transfer was supposed to travel from Jordan to Trinidad to Peru, but Sarkis Soghanalian (an arms trafficker) arranged to have the weapons dropped over Colombia.[88] After this series of incidents was discovered, it eventually contributed to Peruvian President Alberto Fujimore's downfall and the arrest of his intelligence chief, Vladimiro Montesinos. As of this writing, there is no conclusive evidence, at least in the public domain, that a substantial portion of these

---

[85]"Brazil Police Assess Notes on Weapons-for-Drugs Scheme Headed by Beira-Mar," 2001; Lumpe, Lora, ed., *Running Guns: The Global Black Market in Small Arms*, London, UK: Zed Books, 2000, pp. 18–19.

[86]Lumpe, 2000, Chapters 1 and 6.

[87]Tamayo, 2000.

[88]"Gunrunner Sarkis Links Peruvian Army, Sin to Arms Trafficking," 2000.

weapons reached FARC or any other insurgent group in Colombia.[89] However, Colombian authorities have captured two small FARC caches of AK-47s that were traced to the Jordan-Peru shipments.[90]

The second large illegal arms incident occurred in June 2000. As mentioned earlier, a local newspaper reported at the time that the AUC was attempting to bring a large shipment of AK-47s into Barranco Minas.[91]

If this pattern of buying arms in bulk continues, it may have significant strategic and policymaking implications for the United States in regard to Colombia and the entire region.

CONCLUSION

The key finding of the analysis presented in this chapter is that FARC and the AUC are striving for consistency in their arms shipments. These groups are now fighting for control of regions that provide the best access to land and sea routes. Both groups are also beginning to explore relationships with criminal organizations to facilitate larger "bulk" shipments. However, at this time, high-volume purchases are still the exception to the rule. Instead, weapons are trickling into Colombia mostly from Central America through black markets.

Because Colombia's security forces report arms seizures in total numbers, including caches, it is impossible to accurately gauge the volume of arms entering Colombia's internal black market. The number of shipments, however, has increased dramatically—a tenfold increase from 1998 to 2000, and the growth rate was expected to be even greater by the end of 2001. A few hypotheses have been given for this increase: First, some Colombian military authorities attribute the rise in arms shipments to the establishment of FARC's DMZ.[92] Second, FARC itself has also issued statements saying that it planned to heighten both kidnapping and training activities in response to in-

---

[89]See the appendix.

[90]"Authorities Seize Jordanian Arsenal Shipped to Farc," 2000; Tamayo, 2000.

[91]"Traición En El Mercado Negro De Armas," 2000, pp. 1–11.

[92]"Colombia: Navy Seizes Farc Weapons Coming from El Salvador," 1999.

creased U.S. intervention in the form of Plan Colombia.[93, 94] If insurgent groups plan to augment the scale of their training and kidnapping, it is likely that they will need to match this level of commitment with an increase in weapons. Third, the AUC and FARC have both intensified their own cross-fighting to the extent that both groups need more weapons to counteract each other's activities.[95]

The available evidence, however, does not support the first hypothesis. FARC does use its demilitarized zone as a distribution hub, but the DMZ was established in 1998, and the most dramatic increase in arms trafficking didn't begin until late 1999. So, given the time lag, there does not seem to be a strong correlation between the *increase* in arms shipments and the establishment of the DMZ, although the DMZ certainly does provide FARC with the opportunity to stockpile its weapons.

The other two hypotheses follow the arms shipment numbers much more closely. Rumors of Plan Colombia entered into the public debate in the United States and Colombia in the fall of 1999. In the spring of 2000, the FARC Secretariat instructed its fronts to increase their revenue-generating activities to generate approximately $600 million so that FARC could effectively respond to the (Washington-backed) initiative.[96] This time frame also corresponds to more-aggressive attacks by the AUC on traditional FARC-controlled villages. This contextual environment, combined with a dramatic increase in arms trafficking shipments in late 1999, strongly indicates that FARC began to increase its membership and tactical abilities in early 2000 in response to Plan Colombia. Together, the second and

---

[93]"El Otro Plan Colombia," 2000.

[94]According to a U.S. State Department Web site (http://www.state.gov/www/regions/wha/colombia/fs_000719_plancolombia.html), the government of Colombia developed "Plan Colombia" in 1999 as an integrated strategy to meet the most pressing challenges confronting Colombia today—promoting the peace process, combating the narcotics industry, reviving the Colombian economy, and strengthening the democratic pillars of Colombian society. Plan Colombia is a $7.5 billion program.

[95]For a chronology of the intensification of violence in the area, see *Noche Y Niebla: Panorama De Derechos Humanos Y Violencia Politica En Colombia*, Bogotá: Cinep & Justicia y Paz, 2000, p. 18.

[96]"El Otro Plan Colombia," 2000, p. 23.

third hypotheses, therefore, demonstrate a symbiotic relationship between the AUC, FARC, and Colombian security forces.

The U.S. aid package is widely interpreted in Colombia as a state-to-state arms transfer. Because FARC competes with the Colombian security forces for military supremacy, it responded to this state-to-state transfer by purchasing more weapons itself. This stimulated, in turn, an increase in AUC activities to counter FARC, resulting in its own increase in arms procurement.

The next chapter expands on the internal dynamics of Colombia's white, gray, and black markets for small arms. In this expanded discussion, we examine arms trafficking sources and routes that are indigenous to Colombia. Chapter Six, then, returns to the discussion of the internal "arms race" in Colombia and the impact that it is having on Colombian society and the country's prospects for peace.

Chapter Four

PATTERNS OF SMALL-ARMS TRAFFICKING
INSIDE COLOMBIA

The interaction among white, gray, and black markets is even more dynamic after small arms reach Colombia from outside sources. While the previous chapter focused on arms trafficking patterns— i.e., arms sources and trafficking routes—to Colombia, this chapter highlights small-arms trafficking patterns *inside* Colombia.

As mentioned earlier in this report, small arms enter Colombia mostly from black markets in Central America. In the countries neighboring Colombia, the sources and routes are somewhat more diverse, but transactions also tend to take place primarily on the black market. It would therefore be logical to assume that the (*illegal*) weapons coming from various sources are traded almost exclusively on the black market once they reach Colombia. The political conflict in Colombia, however, has matured to the extent that Colombia has developed its own arms sources and trafficking routes independent from those discussed in Chapter Three. An overlap exists between the external and internal markets, and that interaction exacerbates the problem of small-arms trafficking to Colombia.

SOURCES INSIDE COLOMBIA

The reality of the situation in Colombia is that legal and illegal markets for weapons are blended together. This interrelationship makes it almost impossible to separate small-arms availability into white, gray, or black markets. This section attempts to illuminate this problem inside Colombia.

Personal Weapons Sold to Private Citizens

White markets are generally characterized by "transparency" or traceable paperwork that directly links a particular weapon to a buyer and therefore to an authorized user. In Colombia, citizens can purchase personal weapons legally. The military issues these weapons at the request of individual citizens, especially if there is discernible evidence of a threat emanating from a guerrilla group. Unfortunately, Colombia's security forces do not monitor the use of these licensed weapons on a regular basis.[1] This somewhat lax monitoring provides enterprising individuals with the opportunity to sell small arms on the black market.

Members of private security firms also have the opportunity to sell their own legally obtained weapons in the marketplace. Although information is not available in the public domain on the extent of corruption in Colombia's private security firms, Ecuadorian authorities have discovered approximately 22 private security companies (from Quito, Turcan, and Nueva Loja) that are involved in illegal arms trafficking in that country.[2] Additional research is likely to reveal a similar pattern of corruption in Colombia. These weapons, which are obtained from legal sources but moved onto the black market, are not part of the caches in Central America or the arms supplies in the tri-borders area (Argentina, Brazil, and Paraguay). Rather, they represent a completely different source of small arms that is indigenous to Colombia.

Military Weapons Trafficked by Manufacturers and Security Forces

Industria Militar (Indumil) is a Colombian manufacturing company that produces military weapons and ammunition for Colombia's security forces. Authorities have repeatedly uncovered weapons and ammunition from Indumil on the black market and in insurgent groups' caches. These military-style weapons find their way into the hands of insurgents through a variety of sources. Factory workers

---

[1]Author interviews, representative from a local research institute, Bogotá, April 2001.

[2]Simancas, Javier, "Ecuador, 'Santuario' Del Tráfico De Armas," *El País*, July 16, 2000, p. 1.

steal arms and sell them on Colombia's internal market.[3] Weapons storehouses are also frequently raided. In fact, in 1999, small arms were stolen from Indumil storage facilities at least ten times.[4] These munitions could have been taken by workers, guards, military personnel, or even members of FARC, the ELN, or the AUC.

Other black-market sources of military weapons inside Colombia are Colombia's security forces themselves. Indumil manufactures some of these weapons, but others are produced in foreign countries. Local newspapers have reported repeated irregularities in arms supplies within the government's stockpiles. Military personnel who are sympathetic to either the guerrillas or the paramilitaries have been known to supply these groups with military weapons and ammunition. For example, in the fall of 2000, *El Espectador* reported irregularities in the following units' supplies: the 5th Brigade from Bucaramanga, the 4th Brigade from Medellín, the 13th Brigade from Bogotá, and the 12th Brigade in Florencia.[5] Although these reports are unverified, it is interesting to note that in August 2000 a lieutenant in the 13th Brigade was assassinated by members of his unit because they believed that he was engaged in arms trafficking.[6] In another example, Colombian authorities discovered an army employee hiding 50 grenades in her taxi as she traveled in northern Bogotá. The authorities believe that she planned to sell the grenades illegally.[7] These examples demonstrate at least a limited interaction between Colombia's security forces and the internal black market.

It is difficult for one to assess the impact of the white-market and black-market *foreign manufacturing sources* on the entire Colombian small-arms market. As of this writing, weapons from outside sources, such as Central America, overwhelm the internal marketplace. However, paramilitaries and guerrillas apparently use internal sources as stopgap measures to maintain or replace depleted stockpiles. As mentioned in Chapter Three, these groups require a constant supply of weapons and ammunition. While internal sources

---

[3]"Traicion En El Mercado Negro De Armas," *El Tiempo*, June 28, 2000, pp. 1–11.

[4]"El Mercado Negro De Armas Oficiales," *El Espectador*, October 9, 2000.

[5]"El Mercado Negro De Armas Oficiales," 2000.

[6]"El Silencio De Las Armas," *Cambio*, August 14, 2000, pp. 34–37.

[7]"El Mercado Negro De Armas Oficiales," 2000.

may not provide the bulk of the supplies, they can provide insurgents with essential materiel as supplies are running low when external sources are not readily available. Furthermore, the distinction between the military weapons used by Colombia's security forces and the military weapons used by insurgents is not immediately apparent. In addition to its own domestic production, the Colombian government imports weapons from approximately 24 different countries, including Iran, the former Yugoslavia, and South Africa (all of which have a history of being a source of illegal small arms).[8]

To further complicate matters, Indumil manufactures assault rifles that use 5.56-caliber and 7.62-caliber (.51-caliber) ammunition.[9] This fact is significant: It means that there is local production of the ammunition used by both the paramilitaries and the guerrillas. Traditionally, FARC and the ELN have relied on the higher-caliber weapons, while the AUC has employed arms using 5.56-caliber ammunition.[10] Thus, whenever Colombian authorities confiscated a cache of 7.62-caliber rifles and/or shells and bullets, the cache was automatically assumed to have been amassed by a guerrilla group.[11] In the fall of 2000, however, *El País* reported that the AUC was moving toward the Kalashnikov AKM assault rifle. The primary explanation for this move was that it was easier for the paramilitaries to obtain 7.62-caliber (.51-caliber) ammunition than it was for them to obtain lower-caliber ammunition.[12] If this report is true, it appears that the AUC is moving more and more toward *black-market* acquisitions of arms because of increased military pressure on their

---

[8]"Mercado Blanco De Armas." *Cambio*, March 1, 1999, pp. 24–27.

[9]Author interviews, Colombian security officials, Bogotá, June 2001.

[10]Author interviews, Colombian security officials, 2001; "El 'Tumbe' a Las Farc," *Semana*, Internet edition, July 24, 2001 (last accessed July 27, 2001); "Mercado Blanco De Armas," 1999, pp. 34–27.

[11]As mentioned in Chapter Three, from March until August 1999, the Jordanian government sold 10,000 AK-47s to the Peruvian Army and National Intelligence Services. The assault rifles, which were transferred from Jordan to Peru but illegally dumped in Colombia, required 7.62-caliber ammunition. This fact is particularly interesting because, according to reports by the U.S. ATF, the production of 7.62-caliber ammunition is on the decline. In fact, local news reports indicate that this recent acquisition by FARC has not been as beneficial as the group had hoped due to a lack of ammunition supplies.

[12]Author interviews, Colombian security officials, 2001; Rocio Vasquez, Claudia, "42 Vuelos De Trafico De Armas," *El Tiempo*, August 27, 2000, p. 3.

more traditional supply lines. This makes it increasingly difficult to distinguish among those weapons used by paramilitaries, by guerrillas, and by the Colombian security forces because they each use a diversity of military weapons that are produced both internally and externally. Furthermore, these weapons and the ammunition for them are readily available *inside* Colombia, on both the white and black markets.

TRAFFICKING ROUTES INSIDE COLOMBIA

Colombia's internal arms trafficking patterns are relatively sophisticated. The previous section described how the various small arms in Colombia's internal markets become available. That first step in the trafficking pattern takes place in both white and black markets. However, small arms are then recycled through a series of distribution hubs.

The collection and distribution points that are external to Colombia demonstrate some basic trends in the trafficking routes utilized by specific groups. For example, Chapter Three pointed out that the AUC uses ports along the Caribbean coast, while FARC brings weapons in through ports on the Pacific coast of Colombia or on the Gulf of Urabá. Small arms that originate inside Colombia, however, get inserted into distribution hubs from a variety of unidentifiable sources.

In other words, it is not possible to link a particular *internal* source to a specific distribution hub or route as can be done with many external sources and routes. Moreover, once weapons from outside sources enter into Colombia, they intermingle with those already inside the country and are then recycled to insurgents from the same distribution hubs. Further complicating the situation is the fact that ordinary citizens purchase some of these weapons, mostly by tapping into the larger markets in Bogotá, Medellín, and Cali. This disparity of users, sources, and routes results in a complex, fluid, and highly opaque internal market for small arms.

Despite this complicated situation, it is possible to identify three trafficking patterns that do appear to exist in Colombia:

The first route is most directly linked to the ELN. Small arms cross the Venezuelan border through two separate areas: either via water routes down through El Tarra and Convención to Ocaña[13] or through Cúcuta and over land to Pamplona. Each of these crossings feeds directly into Bucaramanga and eventually to Barrancabermeja.

The second route begins in the Gulf of Urabá, near the border with Panama. Like the first route, it contains two access points, in this case the highway through Chigorodó to Dabeiba or the various branches of the Atrato River, traveling upstream again to Dabeiba.[14] From there, the weapons are brought to Medellín for distribution. Most reports attribute the arms trafficking routes from Panama, and particularly from the Gulf of Urabá, to FARC.[15] However, this second route is interesting because Dabeiba is an AUC stronghold.[16] Furthermore, the paramilitaries continue to encroach on FARC along the Pacific coast and in the Chocó Department.[17] These circumstances suggest that the Dabeiba route is most likely utilized by both the AUC and FARC.

The third conduit draws on a patchwork of inner-city trafficking networks in Bogotá. The capital city, like Medellín and Cali, has its own internal black market for small arms. FARC has a strong presence on the periphery of the city, using it as the center of its extortion and kidnapping activities.[18] The black market in small arms is an extension of FARC's presence in Bogotá and the subsequent demand in the city for illegal weapons. Citizens are reportedly able to purchase illegal weapons in the following neighborhoods: San Victorino, El Cartucho, Patio Bonito, Ciudid Bolivar, and Corabastos.[19] The mayor of Bogotá, Antanas Mockus Sivickas, has been working to

---

[13]"La Muerte Al Menudeo," *Semana*, May 3, 1999, pp. 40–47.

[14]"San Andres: Un Paraiso Artificial," *El Tiempo*, October 16, 1994, p. 2B.

[15]"Informe Especial: La Tierra Del Olvido," *Semana*, June 15, 1998, p. 51.

[16]"Colombia, Un 'San Andresito' De Armamento," *El País*, August 22, 2000, p. 2.

[17]"Informe Especial: La Tierra Del Olvido," 1998, p. 51; "Mala Ventura," *Semana*, September 11, 2000, pp. 46–49; McNicholas, Michael, *Colombian Guerrilla and Para-Military Arms Procurement: Origin and Routes*, Panama City: Phoenix Group, 2001.

[18]The authors were able to interview an individual who had conducted seminars and visited communities within these FARC-controlled areas in April 2001.

[19]"El Tráfico De Armas En Bogotá," *El Espectador*, February 7, 2000.

reduce crime in the city, and this effort has had an effect on the availability of small arms. For example, the city is systematically dismantling the El Cartucho neighborhood and creating a city park in the area.[20] If successful, this redevelopment should disperse criminal networks, thereby cutting down on opportunities to sell and purchase weapons on Bogotá's internal black market. Although these changes may make it more difficult for ordinary citizens to purchase small arms on the black market, a system of underground distribution will still exist for more-sophisticated buyers to obtain weapons.

Arms trafficking groups in Bogotá are typically composed of small cells of ten or fewer members. These traffickers either take orders on the streets of the various neighborhoods mentioned earlier or they utilize messenger services to collect and fill more-complicated orders.[21] Large orders are more likely to be delivered in two or three shipments, although sometimes those orders may also be delivered by taxi. This pattern suggests another dimension to the story of the army employee, mentioned earlier in this chapter, who was discovered transporting 50 grenades in a taxi.[22] This woman may have been working independently, but she may also have been a small part of a larger trafficking organization within Bogotá.

CONCLUSION

In this chapter, we discussed the particular problems arms trafficking patterns create for source and transit states. We discussed how the transit routes through Central America and Colombia's neighboring countries contribute to regional instability. These routes contribute to instability indirectly: Traffickers bring corruption, money laundering, and other illegal activities with them as they transverse a country. Trafficking patterns inside Colombia, however, impact the country's political conflict in a much more direct manner.

---

[20]Author interviews with Colombian security officials and with a representative from a local research institute, Bogotá, April and June 2001.

[21]"La Muerte Al Menudeo," 1999.

[22]"El Mercado Negro De Armas Oficiales," 2000.

The fact that both citizens and military personnel insert weapons into the internal black market indicates a broader problem than just insurgents having access to small arms. Sympathizers who supply weapons to guerrillas and paramilitaries represent a relatively simple problem because their motivation for supplying these groups with weapons is likely to be more apparent, and therefore their activities should be relatively easy to trace. Incentives for supplying insurgents with weapons that derive from the desire for profit, however, are far more complex and present a more difficult problem. Indeed, these potential supplies can come from criminal elements with various backgrounds and ideological sympathies, or even from diverse potential suppliers, in the absence of or despite any political sympathies. Because these potential suppliers are diverse, widespread, and idiosyncratic, they indicate a fairly substantial level of corruption in average society. In addition to being an internal source of small arms, ordinary citizens are purchasing illegal weapons on the black market. This situation contributes to the public's demand for guns and illustrates a lack of faith in the government's ability to protect its populace.

Finally and most significantly in this context, the availability and use of small arms is essential to the success or failure of Colombia's insurgent groups. As a result, these organizations continuously contest access to routes inside Colombia. Therefore, not only has the availability of small arms provided insurgents with the means for prolonging Colombia's political conflict, it has also provided an additional motivation for their fighting one another.

Chapter Five

THE WIDER CONTEXT

Small-arms trafficking is a growing international security issue. The patterns of weapons acquisitions, the smuggling routes, and the violence in Colombia all exist within a global context. Morcover, this report's focus on Colombia illustrates how illegal arms trafficking can be viewed as an independent yet significant variable, like narcotics dealing or human smuggling, that contributes to conflict and instability. Thus, in this chapter, we take a step back from our focus on Colombia to explore the problem of illegal arms trafficking in a wider context.

During the Cold War, states provided weapons to their allies and to antagonists alike. The United States, the former Soviet Union, and (to a lesser extent) competing regional powers sometimes used arms transfers to build support for their wider ideological agendas. Small-arms trafficking, therefore, tended to fall into three basic categories: state-to-state weapons transfers, proxy wars, or support to insurgent organizations. As a result, Cold War–era small-arms trafficking was not so much an international security issue as a *national security tool.*

THE CHANGING POLITICAL CONTEXT

In the post–Cold War world, the political context of small-arms trafficking has changed in the following three ways:

First, the United States and Russia no longer dominate the small-arms market.[1] Indeed, governments in Africa, Asia, and Latin America that once received weapons transfers have now increased their own domestic production of small arms. They now supply arms to their security forces and other nations, and sell them to both legitimate merchants and unscrupulous marketeers.[2] Although most of these small-arms transfers are legal, they have expanded and transformed small-arms markets since the Cold War.[3]

Second, small-arms trafficking is now a part of an expanding global marketplace. For example, in its July 2001 *Small Arms Survey*, the United Nations (U.N.) reported that more than 600 companies manufactured small arms worldwide—a threefold increase over the number of manufacturers in 1980.[4] This expansion and privatization of the arms market is a component of an increasingly global economy. New modes of technology in the fields of transportation, communication, and production have allowed small arms to be traded much more fluidly. As a result, the legal trade in small arms has become more complex, making it easier for unscrupulous individuals to hide wholly or partially illegitimate arms trafficking activity within the network of legitimate arms trading. This partly explains why it is so difficult for analysts to accurately determine the volume and dimensions of illegal weapons sales, as in the case of Colombia.[5]

---

[1] Naylor, Thomas, "Gunsmoke and Mirrors: Financing the Illegal Trade," in Lora Lumpe, ed., *Running Guns: The Global Black Market in Small Arms*, London, UK: Zed Books, 2000, pp. 155–178.

[2] Renner, Michael, *Small Arms, Big Impact: The Next Challenge of Disarmament*, Washington, D.C.: Worldwatch Institute, 1997 (available from www.worldwatch.org; last accessed September 19, 2000). This production is sometimes legal, but some countries produce unlicensed AK-47s and M-16s.

[3] Bolton, John R., Undersecretary of Arms Control and International Security, "The Vast Majority of Arms Transfers Are Not Problematic," address to U.N. Conference on Small Arms, *Washington Post*, July 11, 2001.

[4] *Small Arms Survey 2001: Profiling the Problem*, Geneva, Switzerland: United Nations, 2001. Although the total number of arms that are produced has diminished, the proliferation of manufacturers has greatly complicated tracking and monitoring efforts.

[5] Two attributes are fundamental to the notion of globalization of trade: flows of goods and networks of activity. This report acknowledges both attributes as being integral parts of the contemporary small-arms marketplace. As with any other commodity, the movement of weapons into and out of a country affects its geopolitics within a rapidly globalizing, and highly fluid, landscape.

Finally, nongovernmental organizations (NGOs), international relief groups, and activists have framed arms trafficking as a human rights problem.[6] Opponents easily rebut this claim by stating that the problem lies not with the legal availability of small arms but rather with their misuse.[7] Unfortunately, the challenges presented to society by small-arms trafficking are more complicated than either side suggests.

Under the Cold War costs-versus-benefits equation, the benefits of small-arms transfers outweighed the cumulative costs associated with the misuse of those same guns. In the post–Cold War world, three new factors impinge on the small-arms debate: profitability, globalization, and human rights. However, as already suggested, none of these three factors is sufficient on its own to portray small-arms trafficking as an international security issue. Rather, this analysis argues for a new conceptual paradigm that incorporates both old and new thinking about small-arms transfers: Small-arms trafficking is a growing security issue because access to these weapons allows nonstate actors to challenge state authority and power. Furthermore, as these nonstate actors become stronger, their struggle for power rarely remains within a particular state's borders, making small-arms trafficking an international security issue.

THE INTERACTION BETWEEN WEAPONS TRAFFICKING AND POLITICAL VIOLENCE

It is apparent from this study of arms trafficking and Colombia that the influx of small arms into a country or region does not in and of itself cause violent conflict—it is a *symptom* of conflict. Criminals, terrorists, paramilitaries, and guerrillas acquire these weapons because they are easy to obtain, transport, and use.[8] Yet, arms trafficking does

---

[6]The U.N. convened to address this particular issue in July 2001, which was heavily attended by the NGO community.

[7]This is an argument reminiscent of the oft-heard aphorism used by opponents of domestic gun control laws in the United States: "Guns don't kill people, people kill people."

[8]For a discussion on what types of weapons insurgent groups prefer, see Dikshit, Prahant, "Proliferation of Small Arms and Minor Weapons," *Strategic Analysis*, Vol. 17, No. 2, 1994, pp. 189–192.

appear to have contributed to the escalation of violence in Colombia, revealing an important dynamic between weapons trafficking and political violence.

Small Arms as Personal and Military Weapons

The U.S. government defines small arms and light weapons in terms of *military-type use*; therefore, the government definition of small arms includes automatic rifles, machine guns, light mortars, and shoulder-fired missile and rocket systems, but excludes personal weapons.[9] In contrast, NGOs and human rights activists tend to define such weapons by how they affect an individual person's security; therefore, these groups include handguns and land mines in their definition of "small arms."

The analytical problem reflected in this debate over the definition of small arms is that each definition focuses on either the inherent characteristics of small arms or their use. But this distinction does not provide a model for examining the problem discussed here, which is that access to small arms allows nonstate actors to challenge state authority and power. Indeed, our analysis of Colombia revealed that it is difficult, in the context of arms trafficking, to separate the illegal market for handguns from the illegal market for assault rifles in societies in conflict. Thus, the dynamic between weapons trafficking and political violence necessitates an understanding of the problems posed by both small-arms characteristics and small-arms use.

Small Arms as Ideal Smuggling Commodities

Small arms, along with narcotics, diamonds, ivory, and rare wood products, are some examples of commodities traded in illegal markets. Therefore, it is tempting to bundle these items together and view them as presenting inherently the same problem. Although small arms possess a number of characteristics that make them ideal for smuggling, they also possess qualities that are quite distinct from most other forms of illicit merchandise.

---

[9]Bolton, 2001.

Like the other commodities traded in illegal markets, small arms are easy to conceal and transport across borders. Similarly, there is a substantial legitimate small-arms market within which an illicit counterpart can thrive. Unlike some illegal goods (e.g., narcotics), however, small arms are not consumables: They are recycled over and over again in various markets. Personal and military weapons are easily reused because many of them are designed precisely to perform in a wide variety of climates and under numerous types of circumstances.[10] Furthermore, small arms can be used by individuals and/or groups to directly threaten the internal security of a state, further distinguishing them from other nonperishable commodities such as diamonds, ivory, or rare artifacts.

Small Arms as Power Symbols for Insurgent Groups

In addition to the actual use of small arms to challenge states, insurgents frequently view weapons as a means of obtaining power and prestige. For example, decommissioning programs in countries such as El Salvador and Mozambique have revealed reluctance on the part of militias and former combatants to turn in their weapons.[11] This reluctance is based on fears of renewed fighting, but it also stems from the weapons' utility. The weapons can be used for a variety of other purposes, including self-defense, hunting, or banditry.[12] In addition, the prestige invariably associated with possession of a gun, much less a military-issue weapon, is another important factor that limits the effectiveness of voluntary decommissioning programs.

The problems associated with decommissioning weapons are exemplified in what is perhaps the world's most widely publicized decommissioning program: the program that is part of the ongoing peace process in Northern Ireland. Decommissioning in Northern Ireland has become so emotionally charged that it presented a sub-

---

[10]It should be noted, however, that some weapons such as surface-to-air missiles (SAMs) are much more fragile than rifles or handguns and are not as easily concealed.

[11]Arnson, Cynthia, ed., *Comparative Peace Processes in Latin America*, Washington D.C.: Woodrow Wilson Center Press, 1999, pp. 37–57; Dikshit, 1994.

[12]Klare, Michael, and David Andersen, *A Scourge of Guns: The Diffusion of Small Arms and Light Weapons in Latin America*, Washington, D.C.: Federation of American Scientists/Arms Sales Monitoring Project, 1996, pp. 203–213.

stantial obstacle to peace negotiations in 1999 and 2000. The importance to the Irish Republican Army (IRA) of its gun arsenal went beyond just the guns. It represented a "battle cry": An undefeated army does not surrender its weapons. This is a clear example of the *symbolic* power of guns.

Small arms are easy to acquire and use, but they are difficult to give up. This characteristic of small arms illustrates the cause-and-effect relationship between weapons and conflict. Conflict generates a demand for small arms, and the mere possession of such munitions, combined with the power that they represent, makes it far more difficult for combatants to disengage from fighting.

SMALL-ARMS TRAFFICKING USERS, SOURCES, AND ROUTES

The term "arms trafficker" applies to any actor across the spectrum of the illegal arms market, from producer to buyer. An arms trafficker could be the private or public company that manufactures the weapons, the broker who acquires them, the agent who transports them, the buyer (who initially obtains them), the middleman (who moves them), and finally the individual or group who uses them. To add to this complicated scenario, in the case of Colombia, the user (e.g., a security official) may eventually become a seller (albeit an illegal one), prompting the cycle to start all over again, but with an entirely different set of actors and roles those actors are playing, making it difficult to disrupt trafficking patterns.

Users

Users provide the demand for illegal small arms. In the case of Colombia's guerrilla organizations, the users seek to overthrow a particular political state through military-like modus operandi.[13] Notably, the term "guerrilla group" denotes an organization with trained units that conducts reconnaissance and counterintelligence activities and that exercises a level of control over territory. Guerrilla

---

[13]For a discussion on the distinction between terrorists and guerrillas, see Hoffman, Bruce, *Inside Terrorism*, New York: Columbia University Press, 1998, pp. 41–44.

organizations engage mostly in hit-and-run attacks against military or security force targets. Although these organizations often target civilians, they are not the main focus of guerrilla operations.

These characteristics of guerrilla organizations affect their acquisition and use of small arms. In fact, our analysis of FARC revealed that the group requires a substantial quantity of military weapons and ammunition because their members directly confront Colombia's security forces. Guerrillas also have to protect themselves and the territory they occupy, generally by discouraging encroachment by state security forces and intimidating local communities. Therefore, FARC struggles to maintain a continual flow of small arms and ammunition into the organization.

Whereas guerrilla organizations challenge a state's *right* to govern, paramilitary groups, such as the AUC, question a state's *ability* to govern.[14] Indeed, the AUC does not directly confront the Colombian state, but rather presents an alternative that often seems to Colombia's citizens to be a much more viable one. The AUC, through its actions, is essentially saying, "We agree with the states' overall objectives, and we are going to help the Colombian government because it is not strong enough to perform its basic responsibilities on its own." Paramilitary groups may not realize that by presenting themselves as status-quo alternatives to the state, they are in essence challenging the state's authority. In the end, however, both types of subnational groups—guerrillas and paramilitaries—use force to undermine the authority of the state.

To display a show of force, these actors require a certain amount of small arms. As mentioned earlier, weapons that are destroyed or lost need to be replaced, and new recruits require additional armaments. This demand for weapons shapes both the sources of small arms and routes for illegal small-arms trafficking.

It appears from our study that guerrillas and paramilitaries utilize local sources as much as possible for their immediate weapons needs, but are often forced to tap external sources for large volumes of weapons. Our study of Colombia reveals that guerrilla and paramilitary groups also access external sources for more-sophisticated

---

[14]Abrahms, Ray, *Vigilant Citizens*, Cambridge, UK: Polity Press, 1998, p. 8.

weapons, such as shoulder-fired missiles, that might give them a strategic edge over military forces. For example, in the case of FARC, the introduction of Blackhawk helicopters into Colombia presented a new challenge in its struggle against Colombia's security forces; thus, it appears that FARC responded by attempting to acquire surface-to-air missiles (SAMs).

We conclude, therefore, that while the trafficking of most military weapons acts as a useful indicator of guerrilla and paramilitary groups' requirements, tracking of more-strategic weapons provides insight into the groups' overall tactical sophistication and potential expansion.

Sources

Arms sources are not restricted to manufacturers. Sources also include state or military-owned stockpiles, caches, and even underground bazaars. Some insurgents purchase their weapons illegally from the manufacturer, but manufacturers are not the only source of weapons for insurgent groups or paramilitary organizations. Illegal weapons markets in conflict zones, stocks left over from former conflicts, and international criminal organizations all provide insurgents with easy access to small-arms supplies.[15] With such a wide variety of potential sources, user demand works hand-in-hand with ease of availability, causing small arms to flow from conflict zone to conflict zone.[16]

Small arms are purchased in three different markets: white, gray, and black:

The *white market* for military weapons includes weapons bought and sold by authorized private manufacturers or state-owned enterprises. White markets are also the most transparent of the three markets. While small arms are often used by the security forces of an

---

[15]Boutwell, Jeffrey, Michael Klare, and Laura Reeds, eds., *Lethal Commerce: The Global Trade in Small Arms and Light Weapons*, Cambridge, Mass.: American Academy of Arts and Sciences, 1995, pp. 61–113; Sislan, John, and Frederic S. Pearson, "Patterns in Arms Acquisitions by Ethnic Groups in Conflict," *Security Dialogue*, Vol. 29, No. 4, 1998.

[16]Boutwell, Klare, and Reeds, 1995; Sislan and Pearson, 1998.

arms-producing country, some states also transfer military weapons to other nations in the form of aid or as a way of procuring foreign currency. These weapons transfers are legal, so long as they are conducted within the framework of U.N. Security Resolutions or existing multilateral or bilateral treaties, and provided that they are sufficiently documented. White markets also include gun shop owners who purchase personal weapons for resale legally to cash-paying customers. Like the white market for military weapons, the salient characteristic of the white market for personal weapons is transparency: Documents trace the ownership and use of these weapons under the parameters of a given country's laws.

The *gray market* occupies the space between white-market activities and illegal trade in small arms. In the gray market, a state may arrange for an arms transfer to an illegitimate actor (a nonstate actor or a state facing international sanctions) for political or economic purposes, but conceal this transfer within legal channels. Similarly, a manufacturer may *think* that it is selling weapons to a legitimate state/buyer, but is deceived by a middleman who has forged an end-user certificate. In this scenario, a series of intermediaries and transport agents then divert the weapons to a nonlegitimate alternative buyer, such as a guerrilla organization or a state that is subject to international sanctions.

The third source of small arms is the *black market*. Black-market activities are completely illegal. In this case, nonstate actors purchase illicit caches of personal, military, or strategic weapons. The sources for these munitions are as extensive as they are varied and may include munitions siphoned from military stockpiles, stolen from arms manufacturers, procured from criminals, or redirected by private security firms and/or individual gun shop owners.

Notably, the dynamic among these three markets makes it difficult for any one country to address the problem of illegal small arms availability on its own. For example, a weapon may be manufactured and purchased legally, but then resold through the black market. This scenario becomes even more complex when the weapon crosses international borders. This sort of trafficking pattern was startlingly evident in Latin America, demonstrating that source and end-user countries are not the only states affected by small-arms trafficking because smuggling patterns, by necessity, also include countries within the transit routes.

Routes

Arms trafficking routes in and around Colombia present security challenges that are distinct from those associated with arms users or sources. While illegal arms might originate in a source country (e.g., El Salvador), they transit other states (e.g., Panama) on the way to their final destination. This trafficking pattern is also prevalent with the currency used to purchase illegal small arms. Transit states often find themselves indirectly under assault because traffickers bring an underground economy with them wherever they go.

Geography, however, particularly as it pertains to population and topography, clearly impacts trafficking methods and routes more than any other factor. Scarcely populated regions with a limited government presence, such as the border region between Brazil and Colombia, allow traffickers to easily transport commodities in and out of a particular area. Swamps, tributaries, and dense forests also facilitate the covert transport of illegal commodities throughout Latin America. Furthermore, it is evident that even well-guarded seaports can provide traffickers with opportunities for smuggling goods if those seaports handle a sufficiently high volume of legal commerce.[17]

Geography also includes several geopolitical factors that can have an impact on arms trafficking routes. In reality, border states have to work together to maintain security. Indeed, relatively weak states engaged in internal conflict, such as Colombia, place an almost impossibly high burden on their neighbors to police their mutual borders and prevent spillovers of trafficking or violence. Along the same lines, a neighbor of a state targeted by a guerrilla group may actually support insurgents or paramilitary forces by allowing traffickers to use its territory as a distribution hub. Finally, contiguous countries that in the past experienced internal conflict may still be somewhat un-

---

[17]For more information on seaports, smuggling, and the relevance of a high volume of legal commerce, see Flynn, Stephen E., "Beyond Border Control," *Foreign Affairs*, Vol. 79, No. 6, 2000, pp. 57–68.

stable, thereby allowing smugglers easy access to distribution hubs across a border, or those unstable states may ignore the illicit activity entirely.

Arms traffickers also appear to choose transit states with loose import-export restrictions. In many circumstances, the countries we studied are already struggling with other problems such as endemic crime, corruption, poor governance, or chronic violence. In these cases, arms trafficking routes can add yet another burden to the already weak internal security of a transit state.[18] Conduits for smuggling weapons may also negatively impact secure states because illegal weapons that traverse these countries can easily find their way into the hands of local criminal elements or even private citizens. This is especially true if the government in question lacks tight and effective import-export restrictions.

SMALL-ARMS TRAFFICKING AS A USEFUL ANALYTICAL TOOL

In conclusion, it is important to place this study of Colombia and arms trafficking in a wider context. From an analytical perspective, the unique relationship between arms trafficking and political violence makes the study of small-arms trafficking a valuable analytical tool for assessing the extent of a country's domestic stability and measuring the public's confidence in the country's government.

Trafficking patterns not only indicate the strength of a state's internal illegal market, but also provide insight into the state's public institutions and law-enforcement capabilities. For example, a basic responsibility of a nation-state is to protect its populace. If citizens attempt to establish militias or even just procure weapons for personal protection, it would seem to indicate a general belief that the government is incapable of discharging this fundamental responsibility. Militias, therefore, provide a visible metric of governmental authority and credibility and provide an indicator of a decline in that authority and credibility. Moreover, if large numbers of citizens who are not members of militias are also purchasing weapons illegally, this indi-

---

[18]Friman, Richard, "Just Passing Through: Transit States and the Dynamics of Illicit Transshipment," *Transnational Criminal Organizations*, Vol. 1, No. 1, 1995, p. 69.

cates that any fears they may have for their own safety far outweigh any state sanctions or punishment associated with the possession of illegal weapons. It also suggests that citizens are comfortable purchasing items in illegal markets, which may be indicative of an active parallel economy that could eventually threaten the viability of the state in question.

On a more fundamental level, small-arms acquisition and trafficking patterns provide insight into insurgent groups' tactical sophistication, strategic objectives, and political intentions. A combination of an influx of small arms with refugee population flows may serve to pinpoint border regions that traffickers are using for stockpiling illegal weapons and then smuggling them into conflict zones. This combination of an influx of arms and flow of people also suggests that neighboring countries may begin to experience spillovers of violence and economic deterioration as a result of this activity.

Finally, if an insurgent group is purchasing large amounts of military weapons, it casts serious doubts on the possibility of a cease-fire. Similarly, this purchasing activity may indicate that the group is attempting to strengthen its position vis-à-vis the state, via either peace negotiations or military operations. These examples highlight a profound national security problem. While the problem of illegal arms trafficking relates to issues of human rights, underground markets, and even issues of governance, in the end, small-arms trafficking patterns reveal significant gaps in a state's governmental structure and policymaking that may have a direct bearing on the security of the state and its neighbors.

Chapter Six

POLICY IMPLICATIONS

The underlying thesis throughout this analysis is that small-arms trafficking allows nonstate actors to challenge state authority and power, and this thesis certainly held true in our study of Colombia. Our analysis also revealed a dynamic relationship between arms trafficking and political violence. These two conclusions have a number of policy implications for the U.S. government.

IMPLICATIONS FOR INTELLIGENCE ANALYSIS

Significantly, between 1999 and 2001, Colombia's insurgents fought for control of arms trafficking routes. But some observers argue that FARC and the AUC were actually fighting for control over drug distribution centers. For some areas in Colombia, such as Buenaventura, this observation is correct. However, our analysis revealed that FARC and the ELN also use other routes, such as those crossing the border of Ecuador and Venezuela, almost exclusively for transporting supplies. Either way, the insurgents are fighting for control of *routes* rather than just territory. This characteristic of the fighting presents the following intelligence opportunity:

- **Small-arms trafficking patterns pinpoint emerging zones of conflict.**

We concluded that most small arms enter Colombia singly or at most by the dozen rather than by the hundreds or thousands. This "trickle effect" necessitates a constant supply of arms and ammunition to insurgent groups for them to continue their operations. With the increased fighting among Colombian security forces, guerrillas, and paramilitaries, a continual supply of arms represents a real-time strategic requirement. This requirement presents an opportunity for the U.S. intelligence community to gain insight into militant organizations' decisionmaking structures and potential adaptations. Indeed, our study of arms trafficking highlighted the fact that FARC has established elaborate decisionmaking and arms acquisition structures within its organization, enabling consistent processes and proven efficiencies in obtaining weapons.

Small-arms trafficking patterns reveal even more about the AUC than they do about FARC. Once seen as merely a peripheral and reactionary element, AUC has forcibly demanded a role in peace negotiations. Small-arms trafficking patterns have demonstrated that the AUC's strength and sophistication are both increasing, reinforcing the group's demands. In fact, the AUC has begun to compete with FARC over small-arms sources and trafficking routes in Panama and the Caribbean. In addition, the AUC is shifting from smaller 5.56-caliber weapons to larger 7.62-caliber (.51-caliber) weapons, apparently because those larger weapons and the ammunition for them are easier to acquire than smaller-caliber ones.

All of these findings strongly suggest that the AUC is expanding its arms acquisitions beyond its usual sources and, consequently, its capabilities are also expanding. Thus, arms trafficking not only provides insight into the decisionmaking and arms acquisition apparatus of militant organizations, but it also reveals the following weakness in these organizations that potentially can be exploited:

- **Efforts to disrupt a constant stream of weapons into these areas could degrade insurgent groups' overall capabilities.**

One final point in this discussion: Weapons are recyclable, which presents a difficulty in arms trafficking as an analytical tool—insurgents can repeatedly reuse or sell weapons on the black market. Ammunition, although it can be cached, represents a more immediate and more expendable resource requirement and, therefore, is a more accurate real-time indicator of a group's operational strategies.

IMPLICATIONS FOR U.S. FOREIGN POLICY

In the spring of 2000, the U.S. government committed more than $1.3 billion toward Plan Colombia. The aid package, which was originally intended as a measure to counteract drug smuggling out of Colombia, indirectly fanned the flames of the violence in Colombia because insurgent groups interpreted the aid plan as a threat to their continued existence. In response to this threat, the groups stepped up their acquisition of arms. It is clear from recent events (for example, the kidnapping of U.S. Central Intelligence Agency contractors in February 2003) that U.S. aid to Colombia has the potential to shift FARC's activities and attention toward the United States and U.S. interests in the region. This discussion is not meant as a criticism of Plan Colombia per se. Nevertheless, arms trafficking was a contributing factor in the escalation of violence in Colombia between 1998 and 2001. This conclusion has implications for U.S. policy vis-à-vis Colombia and other countries that are experiencing political conflict.

Impact on State Authority

In discussions on U.S. policy toward Colombia, it is necessary to address the concepts of "state authority" and "state power." These terms can be defined broadly and can be applied to varying degrees. This analysis defines authority and power as they exist at a number of societal levels: direct military contests through the application of force and the coercive instruments of the state, citizen behavior with respect to the laws of the land, and interaction between citizens and the state.

In terms of this study, the most obvious displays of state power are Colombia's security forces' skirmishes with guerrilla groups. The military needs decisive victories over FARC, such as the victory in the Juan José, Colombia, battle in August 2001, to build the public perception that the Colombian government is capable of maintaining order.[1] Public perception of this sort will, in turn, help to restore confidence in the government and the populace's acceptance of its

---

[1] News footage from this battle, in which the Colombian armed forces killed approximately 60 rebels and forced the main group of FARC combatants to withdraw from Juan José, was shown on local television news programs in Colombia.

authority. Small arms play a role in this perception of mutually reinforcing authority and power: They are the tools insurgent groups use
to attack Colombia's security forces in an attempt to undermine the
authority of the state and its monopolistic exercise of force.

State authority and power, however, are not derived solely from the
military's ability to win a battle decisively. Just as important to that
authority is a well-defined (and widely accepted) justice system. For
example, every time a citizen pays his or her taxes or modifies his or
her behavior in accordance with the law, governmental authority is
strengthened. Small arms also play a role in this dynamic: Each time
a Colombian citizen purchases or sells a weapon on the black market, he or she weakens the authority of the state by flouting its laws.

Finally, state authority also stems from everyday contact between average citizens and local government representatives, such as the police or mayor. This interaction is extremely important because it
serves to demonstrate that the state exists for the protection and
welfare of its citizens. Small arms play a role even in this derivation of
state authority. Insurgents who walk the streets of rural towns and
small villages displaying their weapons as status symbols institute
their own form of order and authority. Such actions mitigate against
the institution of a strong state authority based on a solid foundation
of ongoing community-government relations.

The access that FARC, the ELN, and the AUC have to small arms has
allowed these groups to directly challenge state authority and power
at every possible level. This was perhaps best reflected in 1998 when
Carlos Castaño, former leader of the AUC, threatened residents of
Puerto Alvira, Meta.[2] Town leaders asked Attorney General Alfonso
Gómez Méndez for protection, but the government failed to respond
to this request.[3] To protect themselves from being caught in the
middle of a violent struggle among FARC, the AUC, and the
Colombian state, community members sent a series of letters to the
government, each of which concluded: "Therefore, we beg the government and the above-mentioned entities to leave on their own ac-

---

[2]"Nación: Tierra Arrasada," *Semana*, May 11, 1998, p. 24.

[3]In 2000, approximately 195 towns did not have a police station. "Cambio De
Guardia," *Semana*, August 7, 2000, pp. 36–38.

cord and to stay away from the town . . ."[4] In effect, the citizens of Puerto Alvira were saying that they could not expect safety or protection from the paramilitaries, the guerrillas, *or* Colombia's security forces. Thus, we draw the following conclusion from this analysis:

- **Small arms allow insurgents to challenge state authority; this, in turn, creates the perception of institutional weakness.**

Effect on Regional Stability

A number of Colombia's elected officials have struggled to solve the problems at the root of Colombia's political conflict. For example, the Betancur Administration (1982–1986) instituted a *Plan Nacional de Rehabilitación*, which redistributed government funds to outlying rural areas of contention that face conflict. Additionally, the Barco Administration (1986–1990) negotiated a peace agreement with the M-19[5] in 1990, including a general amnesty and reinsertion program for M-19 excombatants.[6] Moreover, since the early 1990s, a number of analysts and policymakers have focused on the interrelationship between drugs and conflict in Colombia, arguing that narcotics play a major role in exacerbating the overall complexity and seriousness of political turmoil in the country. However, this analysis of arms trafficking also indicates that the problem of widespread violence is not limited to Colombia. It is tempting to get caught up in the complexity of the conflict in Colombia and miss the wider implications for the entire region. Colombia's neighbors have also been affected by spillover of the conflict, particularly the fighting over trafficking routes. We, therefore, find:

- **Guns—in terms of cross-border spillover of violence—can have as much of a deleterious effect as drugs on the stability of neighboring countries.**

---

[4]"Nación: Tierra Arrasada," 1998, p. 26.

[5]M-19 is another insurgent group operating in Colombia that has renounced violence and has now become a legitimate political group.

[6]Arnson, Cynthia, ed., *Violence in Colombia: Building Sustainable Peace and Social Capital*, Washington, D.C: World Bank, 2000, p. 23; Arnson, Cynthia, ed., *Comparative Peace Processes in Latin America*, Washington, D.C.: Woodrow Wilson Center Press, 1999, pp. 175–182.

Red Herrings and Other Distractions

A number of rumors have surfaced that FARC is trying to acquire shoulder-fired SAMs as strategic weapons. In September 1999, *Semana* published an article titled "The Missiles of the FARC."[7] The article discusses a document sent by the National Association of Excombatants of the FMLN to the U.S. State Department, in which the document's authors claim that FARC purchased 16 SAMs from former FMLN guerrillas.[8] This information should be viewed with some suspicion, however. The National Association of Excombatants has its own internal struggles, and this document could be the result of a power play within El Salvador to discredit the National Association. Interviews we conducted in Colombia could not verifiably substantiate this claim or any other claim pertaining to FARC's acquisition of SAMs.

There has also been an increase in the number of reported cases of drugs-for-weapons swaps between Colombian insurgents and international criminal organizations. The most copiously documented incident was the case of Ferandinho Beira-Mar, who in 2001 arranged with FARC to trade narcotics for guns. Other newspaper reports have cited interactions between Colombia's insurgents and the Russian mafia; Chinese, Mexican, and Israeli criminal gangs; and U.S. drug traffickers. A deeper look into these reports, however, reveals that in most instances a middleman also uses currency to exchange the drugs for the guns. Direct bartering of drugs for guns is rarer than many public news sources would indicate.

The analytical significance of the drugs-for-arms trade is limited. Analysts familiar with the region know that FARC, the AUC, and the ELN are already involved in the drug economy to varying degrees. Agents for each of these insurgent groups reportedly have also been operating in centers for black-market trade such as the cities of Leticia (Colombia), Iguazu Falls (Brazil), and Colón (Panama). We know that insurgents have both available funds and access to criminal organizations through regional black markets, which is the most relevant information in this discussion. The only real significance of

---

[7]"Los Misiles De Las Farc," *Semana*, September 6, 1999, pp. 20–24.

[8]"Los Misiles De Las Farc," 1999.

the drugs-for-guns trade is the moral dilemma that it poses for insurgent groups. All of these groups publicly deny any involvement in the actual production of drugs; therefore, they theoretically cannot exchange cocaine or other drugs for guns. From a policy perspective, whether these groups actually trade cocaine for guns directly or purchase guns with funds derived from cocaine sales is a fine distinction and more of a red herring than an actual arms trafficking pattern.

CONCLUSION

The small-arms trafficking patterns discussed in this report highlight the conceptual limitations of the $1.3 billion U.S. funding of Plan Colombia and other similar policies. The primary weakness, as it relates to the United States, is that the aid package did not help Colombia address its problem of diminishing authority in the face of increased aggressive behavior by insurgents. Our research indicates a strong correlation between an increase in arms trafficking and U.S. military assistance to the Colombian government, which, in turn, appears to have stimulated an escalation in violence as nonstate actors have fought for control of trafficking routes. This cycle of violence illustrates how difficult it is to focus on one element of conflict in Colombia, in this case, drug trafficking apart from other related problems. Moreover, the assistance package did not help to alleviate the spillover of security threats from Colombia to other countries in the region, which was also revealed by an examination of small-arms trafficking patterns.

In addition to these direct implications for U.S. policy in the region, this study also revealed that arms trafficking patterns are useful analytical tools. They provide insight into the likely intentions of militant organizations and how group objectives may be changing. Arms trafficking patterns also provide insight into the tactical capabilities of militant groups. This finding is particularly relevant as it relates to patterns of ammunition acquisition. Finally, trafficking patterns can provide insight into the internal dynamics of a state, especially with regard to state authority. As such, arms trafficking patterns are useful analytical tools for intelligence analysts and policymakers alike.

RESEARCH METHODOLOGY

The objective of this study was to explore small-arms trafficking patterns into and within Colombia using open-source information exclusively: i.e., newspapers, magazines, journals, seminars, and interviews with individuals in the region. In conducting this research, RAND staff collected more than 500 newspaper, magazine, and journal articles, approximately 200 of which included reports of small-arms interdictions and arms caches that were uncovered.

The research problem, therefore, was not necessarily finding the information we needed, but rather filtering through the available sources to isolate consistent and verifiable arms trafficking patterns. To do this, RAND first created a database of information and articles on small-arms trafficking into and within Colombia. The types of information included in the data set that RAND developed included the following: arms origin, shipping method, transit route, interdiction country, middleman, end-user certificate, black market, number and type of weapons, amount and type of ammunition, and suspicious activity labeled "other." With one or two exceptions, the data set date begins on January 1, 1998, and ends on August 31, 2001.

To verify this information, we conducted three separate research trips to the region. The first trip was to Argentina, the purpose of which was to explore the importance of small-arms sources in the southern cone of the region and specifically in the tri-borders area of Argentina, Brazil, and Paraguay. We also traveled to Colombia on two separate occasions. In April 2001, we interviewed local citizens working toward conflict resolution, leaders of well-respected local NGOs, journalists, and academics. The purpose of that trip was to balance newspaper reports with stories of what the Colombian people were actually experiencing in these areas controlled by FARC, the ELN, and the AUC. In June 2001, we returned to Colombia to interview intelligence officers, military and security people, city officials, and representatives from the U.N. The purpose of that trip was to find answers to certain questions that we felt were suspiciously answered in the written documents or were not answered clearly. For reasons of personal security, the interviewees have requested that they not be cited, acknowledged, or thanked specifically in this report.

Footnoted citations in this report telling readers to see this appendix indicate that our analysis was culled from or informed by the entire RAND data set—verified by local interviews—and not just from one or two specific sources. Similarly, we have attempted to draw attention to specific information that was gleaned from our interviews in the region and that cannot be found in published documents.

Finally, RAND supplemented this information with primary research support provided by the Phoenix Group, a private security and investigative firm operating in the Republic of Panama (any information provided by the Phoenix Group is attributed to the firm in this report). As with our trip to the southern cone, the purpose of this research was to obtain information on patterns of arms trafficking from Central America into Colombia. The Phoenix Group works with the government of Panama and private companies to track legal shipments of goods to prevent them from being used by smugglers to transport illegal goods—primarily drugs—in and around Panama. As such, the Phoenix Group used its preexisting knowledge to generate a report for RAND on ports in the waters connecting Central America and Colombia and patterns of illegal shipping into and out of those ports. RAND researchers attempted to verify this information through a review of additional open-source documents and by conducting interviews.

RAND researchers also attended two informative conferences—one conducted by the Center for Naval Analysis in October 2000 titled "Colombia: Strategic End-State Goals and Means" and one conducted by the Atlantic Council in December 2000 titled "Toward a Comprehensive Strategy for Addressing the Crisis in Colombia"—to gain insight into U.S. policy issues surrounding arms trafficking and Colombia.

BIBLIOGRAPHY

Abrahms, Ray, *Vigilant Citizens*, Cambridge, UK: Polity Press, 1998.

"Armas Por Coca," *Cambio*, July 12, 1999, pp. 30–31.

"Arms Trafficking to Colombia Increases," *El Comercio*, August 23, 2000.

"Army Reports Heavy Child Involvement in Guerrilla War," *El País*, December 27, 2000.

Arnson, Cynthia, ed., *Comparative Peace Processes in Latin America*, Washington, D.C.: Woodrow Wilson Center Press, 1999.

Arnson, Cynthia, ed., *Violence in Colombia: Building Sustainable Peace and Social Capital*, Washington, D.C.: World Bank, 2000, p. 23.

"Authorities Seize Ammunition Shipment in Border Area," *El Nacional*, September 29, 2000.

"Authorities Seize Jordanian Arsenal Shipped to Farc," Bogotá: Caracol Colombia Radio, FBIS-LAT-2000-1216, 2000.

Bedoya Lima, Jineth, "La Autopista De Las Farc En Plena Selva," *El Espectador*, April 27, 2001.

"Bloque De 25 Paises Contra El Mercado Negro De Armas," *El Tiempo*, May 8, 1998, p. 1.

Bolton, John R., Undersecretary of Arms Control and International Security, "The Vast Majority of Arms Transfers Are Not Problematic," address to U.N. Conference on Small Arms, *Washington Post*, July 11, 2001.

Boutwell, Jeffrey, and Michael Klare, eds., *Light Weapons and Civil Conflict: Controlling the Tools of Violence*, New York: Rowman & Littlefield, 1999.

Boutwell, Jeffrey, Michael Klare, and Laura Reeds, eds., *Lethal Commerce: The Global Trade in Small Arms and Light Weapons*, Cambridge, Mass.: American Academy of Arts and Sciences, 1995.

"Brazil Police Assess Notes on Weapons-for-Drugs Scheme Headed by Beira-Mar," *Zero Hora*, March 15, 2001.

"Brazil's 'Pablo Escobar' Exchanged Arms for Drugs with Farc," *El Espectador*, February 20, 2001.

"Cambio De Guardia," *Semana*, August 7, 2000, pp. 36–38.

Chauvin, Lucien, and Juan Tamayo, "Peru, Colombia Want U.S. to Resume Anti-Drug Support," *Miami Herald*, August 4, 2001.

Clinton Administration Aid Proposal, Internet edition, Center for International Policy, January 11, 2000 (available from www.ciponline.org/colombia/aidprop2.html; last accessed March 1, 2000).

"Colombia, En La Mira," *El Tiempo*, electronic archives, June 28, 2001 (last accessed July 5, 2001).

"Colombia: Navy Seizes Farc Weapons Coming from El Salvador," *Paris AFP*, January 4, 1999.

"Colombia, Un 'San Andresito' De Armamento," *El País*, August 22, 2000, p. 2.

"Das Seizes Smuggled Nicaraguan Military Rifles," Bogotá: Caracol News, FBIS-LAT-2000-6010, 2000a.

"Das Seizes Smuggled Nicaraguan Military Rifles," Foreign Broadcast Information Service, Santa Fe Caracol Television, June 1, 2000b (restricted online news service; last accessed November 20, 2000b).

Delgado, Naya, "Panama Becomes Bazaar for Central American Weapons," *Reuters*, Internet edition, April 21, 2000 (last accessed September 25, 2000).

"Desactivan Dos Carros Bomba En Barrancabermeja," *El Tiempo*, May 25, 2001.

Dikshit, Prahant, "Proliferation of Small Arms and Minor Weapons," *Strategic Analysis*, Vol. 17, No. 2, 1994, pp. 187–204.

Dyer, Geoff, "Time Bomb at Brazil Outpost," *Financial Times*, Internet edition, October 3, 2000 (available from www.ft.com; last accessed October 4, 2000).

"El Amigo De Jojoy," *Cambio*, November 6, 2000, pp. 18–28.

"El Gobierno De Las Farc," *Semana*, January 25, 1999, pp. 23–27.

"El Mercado Negro De Armas Oficiales," *El Espectador*, October 9, 2000.

"El Otro Plan Colombia," *Cambio*, March 20, 2000, pp. 23–27.

"El Silencio De Las Armas," *Cambio*, August 14, 2000, pp. 34–37.

"El Sur, 'Paraíso' De Traficantes De La Guerra," *El País*, May 7, 2000.

"El Tráfico De Armas En Bogotá," *El Espectador*, February 7, 2000.

"El 'Tumbe' A Las Farc," *Semana*, Internet edition, July 24, 2001 (last accessed July 27, 2001).

"Farc Retains Cars, Demands Ransom in Northwestern Colombia," *Paris AFP*, December 28, 2000.

"Farc Se Movilizan Al Sur De Bolívar," *El Tiempo*, July 16, 2001.

Ferraz, Silvio, "Armed Forces Mobilize in Response to Farc," *Sao Paulo Veja*, November 10, 1999.

Flynn, Stephen E., "Beyond Border Control," *Foreign Affairs*, Vol. 79, No. 6, 2000, pp. 57–68.

"Four Days in the City of Terror," *Ma'ariv*, October 7, 1994, pp. 2–5.

Franco, Ilimar, "Pf to Block Farc Supply Routes in Amazon," *Jornal do Brasil*, August 20, 1999.

Friman, Richard, "Just Passing Through: Transit States and the Dynamics of Illicit Transshipment," *Transnational Criminal Organizations*, Vol. 1, No. 1, 1995, pp. 65–83.

"General Tapias on Puerto Lleras Attack," *Semana*, FBIS Reprint FTS19990720001608, July 11, 1999.

"Gunrunner Sarkis Links Peruvian Army, Sin to Arms Trafficking," *Lima La Republica*, September 21, 2000.

Held, David, Anthony McGrew, David Goldblatt, and Jonathan Perraton, *Global Transformations: Politics, Economics and Culture*, Cambridge, UK: Polity Press, 1999.

Hoffman, Bruce, *Inside Terrorism*, New York: Columbia University Press, 1998.

"Incautadas Quince Mil Armas En Cinco Años," *El País*, July 11, 2000, p. 1.

"Informe Especial: La Tierra Del Olvido," *Semana*, June 15, 1998, pp. 48–53.

Jenkins, Brian Michael, "Colombia: Crossing a Dangerous Threshold," *The National Interest*, 2000, pp. 47–55.

Klare, Michael, and David Andersen, *A Scourge of Guns: The Diffusion of Small Arms and Light Weapons in Latin America*, Washington, D.C.: Federation of American Scientists/Arms Sales Monitoring Project, 1996.

"La Batalla De Antioquia," *Cambio*, May 24, 1999, pp. 32–35.

"La Guerrilla Nunca Fue Como La Imaginábamos," *El Espectador*, April 27, 2001.

"La Muerte Al Menudeo," *Semana*, May 3, 1999, pp. 40–47.

"La Paz Sobre La Mesa," *Cambio*, Special Edition, May 11, 1998, pp. 20–65.

"Las Finanzas De Los Paras," *Cambio*, May 15, 2000, pp. 14–21.

Laurance, Edward, and William Godnick, "Weapons Collection in Central America: El Salvador and Guatemala," in *Managing the Remnants of War: Weapons Collection and Disposal as an Element of Peace-Building*, Bonn, Germany: Bonn International Center for Conversion, 2000.

Leal, Jimenez, "Arms, Drug Trafficking on Pacific Coast," *El Colombiano*, November 7, 1999.

Lock, Peter, "Breaking the Cycle of Violence: Light Weapons Destruction in Central America, in *BASIC PAPERS* series, London, UK: British American Security Information Council, 1997.

"Los Costos Del Cese Al Fuego," *El País*, July 6, 2000, p. 1.

"Los Misiles De Las Farc," *Semana*, September 6, 1999, pp. 20–24.

"Los Planes De Las Farc," *Semana*, August 7, 2000, pp. 34–35.

Lumpe, Lora, ed., *Running Guns: The Global Black Market in Small Arms*, London, UK: Zed Books, 2000.

Lunazzi, Eduardo, "San Andres Se Pone En Guardia," *El Tiempo*, October 16, 1994, p. 21A.

Lunazzi, Eduardo, "San Andres, Puente De Armas Y Narcotrafico Dice Mindefensa," *El Tiempo*, October 15, 1994, p. 7A.

"Mala Ventura," *Semana*, September 11, 2000, pp. 46–49.

Marcella, Gabriel, *Plan Colombia: The Strategic and Operational Imperatives*, Carlisle, Pa.: Strategic Studies Institute, 2001.

Martins, Marco Antonio, "Two of Beira-Mar's Girlfriends Still Evade Police," *Jornal do Brasil*, February 20, 2001.

Mauricio Vega, Carlos, "La Caldera Del Diablo," *Cambio*, November 20, 2000, pp. 53–56.

McDermott, Jeremy, "Welcome to Farclandia," *BBC News*, Internet edition, January 13, 2001 (available from http://news.bbc.co.uk; last accessed July 17, 2001).

McNicholas, Michael, *Colombian Guerrilla and Para-Military Arms Procurement: Origin and Routes*, Panama City: Phoenix Group, 2001.

"Mercado Blanco De Armas," *Cambio*, March 1, 1999, pp. 24–27.

"Mercado Negro A Pesar Del Desarme," *El Tiempo*, August 2, 1999.

"Militares Venezolanos Entrenaron Al Eln," *El Tiempo*, March 29, 2001.

"Nación: Tierra Arrasada," *Semana*, May 11, 1998, pp. 24–27.

National Drug Control Strategy, Internet edition, Washington, D.C.: Office of National Drug Control Policy, 2001 (available from www. whitehousedrugpolicy.gov/publications/policy/ndcs01/index. html; last accessed August 6, 2001).

Naylor, Thomas, "Mafias, Myths, and Markets: On the Theory and Practice of Enterprise Crime," *Transnational Criminal Organizations*, Vol. 3, No. 3, 1997, pp. 1–45.

Naylor, Thomas, "Gunsmoke and Mirrors: Financing the Illegal Trade," in Lora Lumpe, ed., *Running Guns: The Global Black Market in Small Arms*, London, UK: Zed Books, 2000, pp. 155–178.

Noche Y Niebla: Panorama De Derechos Humanos Y Violencia Politica En Colombia, Bogotá: Cinep & Justicia y Paz, 2000, p. 18.

O'Neill, Bard E., *Insurgency and Terrorism: Inside Modern Revolutionary Warfare*, Washington, D.C.: Brassey's Inc., 1990.

Padilla, Nelson Freddy, "Cabañuelas De Paz," *Cambio*, December 21, 1998, pp. 24–25.

"Panamá, Ruta Preferida Por Traficantes," *El Espectador*, September 10, 2000, p. 2.

Penhaul, Karl, "Colombia's Communist Guerrillas Take on Feminine Face," *Boston Globe*, Internet edition, January 7, 2001 (available from www.boston.com; last accessed January 9, 2001).

Perfil Maritimo De America Latina Y El Caribe, New York: United Nations, CEPAL LC/W.001 Rev. 2, 2001 (available from www.eclac.cl/transporte; last accessed August 1, 2001).

Plan Colombia: Plan for Peace, Prosperity, and the Strengthening of the State, United States Institute for Peace Online Library, Bogota, Colombia: Presidency of the Republic, May 15, 1999 (available from www.usip.org/library/pa/colombia.adddoc/plan_colombia_101999.html; last accessed August 6, 2001).

"Plan Desarme Llegó a Palmira," *El Pais*, June 17, 2000.

Quirk, Peter, "Money Laundering: Muddying the Macroeconomy," *Finance and Development*, 1997, pp. 7–9.

Rabasa, Angel, and Peter Chalk, *Colombian Labyrinth: The Synergy of Drugs and Insurgency and Its Implications for Regional Stability*, Santa Monica, Calif.: RAND, MR-1339-AF, 2001.

Rana, Swadesh, *Small Arms and Intra-State Conflicts*, New York: United National Institute for Disarmament Research, 1995, p. 34.

Renner, Michael, *Small Arms, Big Impact: The Next Challenge of Disarmament*, Washington, D.C.: Worldwatch Institute, 1997 (available from www.worldwatch.org; last accessed September 19, 2000).

"Reports Say Traffickers Made Five Flights to Deliver Russian Arms," *Madrid EFE*, September 3, 2000.

Ríos Rojas, Julian, "El Arsenal De Farc Y Eln," *El Espectador*, August 27, 2000, p. 2.

Rocio Vasquez, Claudia, "42 Vuelos De Trafico De Armas," *El Tiempo*, August 27, 2000, p. 3.

"Salida Al Mar," *Cambio*, May 31, 1999, pp. 34–35.

"San Andres: Un Paraiso Artificial," *El Tiempo*, October 16, 1994a, p. 2B.

"San Andres, Un Paraiso Artificial (Part II)," *El Tiempo*, October 17, 1994b, pp. 1A–3A.

"Se Destapan Cartas Sobre Cese Al Fuego," *El Espectador,* Internet edition, July 23, 2001 (last accessed July 23, 2001).

Selsky, Andrew, "Colombian Rebel Unit Routed in Ground, Air Counterattack," *Miami Herald,* August 3, 2001.

Serafino, Nina M., *Colombia: Conditions and U.S. Policy Options,* Washington D.C.: Congressional Research Service, RL 30330, 1999.

Simancas, Javier, "Ecuador, 'Santuario' Del Tráfico De Armas," *El País,* July 16, 2000, p. 1.

Sislan, John, and Frederic S. Pearson, "Patterns in Arms Acquisitions by Ethnic Groups in Conflict," *Security Dialogue,* Vol. 29, No. 4, 1998, pp. 393–408.

Small Arms Survey 2001: Profiling the Problem, Geneva, Switzerland: United Nations, 2001.

Tamayo, Juan, "Peru's Link to Arms Deal Worried U.S.," *Miami Herald,* September 20, 2000.

Toward Greater Peace and Security in Colombia: Forging a Constructive U.S. Policy, New York: Council on Foreign Relations and the Inter-American Dialogue, 2000.

"Traición En El Mercado Negro De Armas," *El Tiempo,* June 28, 2000, pp. 1–11.

UNHCR (United Nations High Commissioner for Refugees) 2000 Mid-Year Progress Report, Geneva, Switzerland: United Nations, 2000.

UNHCR 2001 Global Appeal–Strategies and Programmes, Geneva, Switzerland: United Nations, 2001.

Villaveces, Andres, Peter Cummings, Victoria E. Espitia, Thomas D. Koepsell, Barbara McKnight, and Arthur L. Kellermann, "Effect of a Ban on Carrying Firearms on Homicide Rates in Two Colombian Cities," *Journal of the American Medical Association,* Vol. 283, No. 9, 2000, pp. 1205–1209.

Violence in Colombia: Building Sustainable Peace and Social Capital, Washington, D.C.: World Bank, 2000.

Wilson, Scott, "Colombia's Other Army," *Washington Post*, March 12, 2001a.

Wilson, Scott, "Interview with Carlos Castano, Head of the United Self-Defense Forces of Colombia," *Washington Post*, March 12, 2001b.

Wood, Brian, and Johan Peleman, *The Arms Fixers: Controlling Brokers and Shipping Agents*, Oslo: Norwegian Initiative on Small Arms Transfers, 1999.